THE PRIDE OF t20 CRICKET

A Novel by

Abhishek Kapoor

ISBN 978-93-5396-585-3

AUTHOR'S MESSAGE

"Thank you for loving my previous book so much.

The Selfish Betrayals was a visual representation of thrilling scenes using the magic of words. The Pride of t20 cricket is not only hilarious but also a quick read that aims to bring a smile on your face.

I dedicate this novel to my 2020 born little one!"

-   **Abhishek Kapoor**

Scan the code below to get in touch with him

Send an email to writetokapoor@hotmail.com

CONTENTS

NOTE

Though the plot is **not at all linked** to The Selfish Betrayals, there are a few characters and locations that reappear.

There is no compulsion to go through the previous novel as this is **not a sequel**. In fact, it is **totally independent** and if any reader has not read The Selfish Betrayals, he/she can still follow the plot with utmost ease.

Following are the list of characters that reappear:

Master Shams-ud-din: In his late forties, he is the most skilled and overpriced tailor of Kanpur and the owner of The Powerful Horse Boutique.

Hargurjeet Singh: Son of a business tycoon and a former MLA, he is known for his rapper like accent and luxurious lifestyle.

Anjana Chatterjee Singh: The former girlfriend of Hargurjeet is now his wife.

Gardner: An old man who works at Hargurjeet's farm.

Monty C Dhingra: Now thirty two, he is a private investigator who returns after a successful rehabilitation post imprisonment for accidental drug abuse.

Rita Mishra: Monty's domestic employee.

Sarfaraz: A young tailor who works at The Powerful Horse boutique.

Sooraj Singh: A notorious cab driver who lives with his wife and two children.

Scarlett White (mention only): The well known model of Kanpur whose murder case Monty investigated.

Following are the list of locations that reappear:

Hargurjeet Singh's farm: Located just outside Kanpur, away from the noise but not air pollution.

Shakuni Children's Park: A park opposite to Scarlett's mysterious bungalow in Tilak Nagar, Kanpur.

Monty's 1BHK flat: Located on the first floor of a posh apartment in a posh locality.

1

THE RIDICULOUS CONTROVERSY

Sunday, 23/June/2019

The fanatical excitement was at its peak. And why would it not be? The final of Kanpur's most prestigious Incredible Cricket Championship 2019 between the top two teams of the tournament, Southern Blasters and Officers XI, had meandered like a sine curve into the second half of its final over and still there was no clear winner. The Officers needed only four more runs to win of the last three balls. Though they still had the luxury of five wickets in hand but considerable tension was clearly evident on the faces of their players in the dugout.

Not only the fielders and the left arm pacer, but also the batsmen, the umpires and even the spectators were totally drenched with sweat. It was indeed a hot and humid June afternoon that Sunday.

The paunchy fifty five year old Sikh and one of the most reputed cricket coaches in the town, Mr. Canada Singh, happened to be the coach of the bowling team. Some may believe that shouting, sledging and cursing was against his character, but the stage of the match was such that the Punjabi genes in him had no other option but to get activated.

The fourth delivery of the over was an attempt to severely injure or perhaps even kill the batsman. A bouncer angling right into the jaw but the poor fellow somehow managed to duck under it. A dot ball none the less, taking the match even closer than what everyone expected. The bowler, a bearded six feet Jaat, reached near the batsman in his giant follow through and said, "Rarely do I misfire." He had probably seen the shock register on his target's face before the latter could hide it.

"Ah, that was a good fluke but don't try it again," heard the fierce bowler from behind. The voice was deep yet vibrating with power and command. It was indeed the coach Mr. Canada Singh. One of the fielders had collapsed on the boundary, perhaps due to the combination of heat, dehydration and pressure. While the physiotherapist was checking the player, the coach made his way to the middle of the ground.

The bowler did not appreciate this at all as it foiled his attempt to set the batsman up for the next delivery. Even before he could respond, the umpire intervened, "Coaches are not allowed in the playing area. Get out of here."

"Shut up for a minute, you parsimonious ladies' tailor. Balloo, my boy, you need to bowl a slower one outside off. He will try to go after it on the next ball. You have to deceive him. Remember my words." The coach was louder than he should have been. The non striker heard it and rushed towards the striker to reveal the cleverly intricate bowling plan to him.

"I told you to get out of here. You are an experienced man and look your fielder is up too," said the bearded umpire, Master Shams-ud-din adjusting his Mahatama Gandhi style spectacles below the white hat.

"Tailor Master, I do not think that you can ever improve your aberrant habit of unnecessarily poking your pointed nose everywhere. Sorry for the interruption. I will leave now." He jogged out of the playing area leaving the umpire red faced.

If Balloo was smart, he would have realized that the batsman was obviously aware of the bowling plan for the next delivery and would have then changed it accordingly. But, Balloo was actually one of those rich law students who have a reserved seat in the college not due to their talent but only because of their ancestor's surname.

As expected, the second last ball was right in the slot at a pace that any spinner would be proud of; but not the turn. The batsman's eyes lit up and he stepped across dragging it from outside off to over cow corner fence for a monster six with the ball landing several rows back into the crowd that had gathered to witness the decisive match.

It was a defeat for the Southern Blasters but a bereft of the ignominy because of the fact that they came so close to winning the title. The Officers were jubilant and so were their supporters. There were some disappointed faces on the Blasters' side but none more than the head coach. Canada Singh had worked harder than anyone else to win the tournament. His ardent aspirations shattered just like the previous eight years.

"Perhaps winning this title will always be my unfulfilled dream," he murmured. There is always a sort of broken hearted that is akin to lightning a match, enjoying the flame and leaving the ashes. Canada's memories of the all nine years of the tournament were like that flame. A spark every year would give him hope that he could win it and then it turned into ashes which he watched getting blown away by the mournful wind.

"Well played boys. The result is a matter of destiny, what matters the most is that we tried our best," he said like every other coach would to the dejected players of his team. The fire in his black eyes seemed totally drowsed by icy water. The players too appeared to be in disappointment that was too much to cope up with at that moment. A couple of them even had teary eyes.

"Welcome to the post match presentation ceremony," said Master Shams-ud-din, the umpire turned anchor. Surprisingly, he had changed his attire from the white hat and black shirt-trouser to his usual green turban and white kurta-pyjama. The press had gathered to cover the event and all their cameras were already on. Even the organizers and other dignitaries had taken their place on the stage.

He continued, "Congratulations to the new champions. In the last seven years of umpiring, never have I ever seen a coach run into the playing area at the time when the match is going on. But it happened today. As an umpire, I could have awarded five penalty runs to the Officers at that very moment. In that case, the match would have ended without any more deliveries being bowled. But I thought that the entire team should not be punished for a ridiculous mistake committed by a man in pure excitement. After the last ball six, I realized that it was not a juvenile mistake. Instead it was a well thought trick. He wanted his own team to lose the match. He instructed his fielder to act and the innocent bloke just collapsed on the boundary to pause the match for some minutes. Then this zealous coach ran into the playing area and in his loudest, clearest voice told the bowler how to bowl the next delivery, making sure that the batsmen comfortably hear the plan. Canada is such an extra ordinarily clever man that not only the players of his own team, but also the batsmen of the opposite team could not realize that he is the one betraying all of them. Maybe he got loads of bucks from the illegal bookies for cheating in this manner, maybe some other benefits but whatever he did is not acceptable at all. I would request the organizers and team owners to ban this immoral, unethical and dishonest man from coaching any team in this prestigious tournament next year onwards. We will now proceed to the prize distribution ceremony."

Hundreds of cameras accompanied by thousands of eyeballs turned towards Canada Singh. The coach under suspicion had prepared a greeting smile for the post match presentation ceremony but obviously none could make its way on his cylindrical face. Almost robotically, he raised his hands up, closing his eyes as if he was a dreadfully violent wanted criminal surrendering himself to the police. Though half covered with the salt and pepper hair of his beard, his maroon lips turned blue even in the heat of June and his feet moved slowly towards his team in a strange manner as if any inexperienced person was controlling them using a remote. His brain formulated no other thoughts but to register that he was brutally shocked. Slowly, he opened his eyes keeping his mouth closed and looked straight at his white shoes.

"Why did you cheat?"

"Who paid you?"

"Is any player involved in this scandal?"

"For how long have you been cheating?"

"Are you not ashamed?"

The journalists fired all sorts of questions towards the losing coach, paying almost no attention to the man of the match and man of the series prizes being distributed on the stage. They got a spicy headline for their respective media houses. Who cares what happens in the world? Who cares how many people die in protests? Who cares how many roads were made in the last month? Who cares about the GDP of the nation? All they care about is the TRP they would get by covering airport dresses of celebrities or cricket scandals like the one that they just witnessed.

When a human sees something inappropriate in front of his eyes, his anger boils up and after a certain limit of tolerance, it converts into rage. The wise spectators, including those who had no clue of what had just happened, got the opportunity to jump over the grill and run onto the field to team up with the media persons to shout anti-Canada Singh slogans. And when things get out of control, they get ugly too.

A powerful push from the back almost took the silent coach down face first on the ground but the one from the front was equal in force, therefore managed to balance out the resultant force to prevent the great fall. Even in rage, people did not forget to respect religion. None of the smacks at the back of his neck and head were aimed at his blue turban.

Before there was a broken nose or a broken leg, Balloo and his teammates pulled their coach into the dressing room and locked the door. Some people from the press thought that the entire team would beat him up for betraying them, while others opinioned that the players would just interrogate him.

"I did not do it. That tailor has lied," said the teary eyed Canada, surrounded by his own squad, just like the cruel, remorseless vultures surround the lifeless bodies of the stooges at the end of a bloody and memorable battle.

But, they were the Southern Blasters, not real vultures. They had at least the minimum respect that every student should have for his teacher. A team is successful only when it works as a unit and not as a set of individuals. They had learnt it from their coach and it was the time for them to protect him from the unthinking mob.

"Sir, each one of us believes you. It was just a mistake you made in excitement. This is not the time to discuss. We can do that later. The back door is safe to get away," replied Zorawar, the captain and the record breaking batsman of the tournament. And that was precisely the exit which Canada took to mysteriously disappear from the stadium amidst the chaos.

2

ANNUAL PRESS CONFERENCE

Friday, 14/February/2020

At Hargurjeet Singh's farm

One of the security guards announced that the press conference had been delayed by twenty minutes due to unavoidable circumstances. Perhaps the discussion inside the single storey farmhouse failed to be a brief one. After all when there are over a dozen officials and a couple of outsiders involved, it does take more time than expected to mutually agree on paramount issues. The journalists however were in no mood to complain. They were being treated royally by the well dressed and attentive waiters, who had been specially arranged for the much anticipated annual event.

"The apple juice is fantastic," said one of the journalist in a safari suit to Canada Singh, who himself was anxiously waiting for the proceedings to commence.

"Yes, it is," he replied and then he quickly lowered his eyes and walked towards the opposite side, attempting to straighten his pale white t-shirt's collar, although it was completely covered by the black blazer.

Canada did not want to engage in any sort of conversation with anybody till the official declaration was made regarding his future. He knew that most of them wanted to report random humiliating stuff regarding him and he was not there to provide them content. Therefore, he sat on a chair, all lone at the corner, with the practical vision similar to that of a ridden horse, the stage being the only target of his eyes and ears.

The journalists took their chairs like gas fills an empty cylinder, leaving no space at all for some of their counter parts as the officials walked out, one by one through the wooden door. Dressed in a navy blue suit complimenting his red turban, the chairperson, Hargurjeet Singh took his seat in the middle and the others to his left and right.

Carrying the blue Banarsi saree elegantly, Anjana seemed too happy as she sat next to her husband. She was probably the only woman in the entire farm at that moment and she seemed to enjoy the apparent attention. The other office bearers had put on an absolutely unneeded smile. On the other hand, the owners of the Southern Blasters and their handsome captain Zorawar joined the group of standing journalists as there were no empty chairs left for them.

A wireless microphone was already arranged for chairman and he began addressing the group in his usual Punjabi rapper like accent, "Welcome, welcome, welcome. Today we had a board meeting and with mutual consent of all members, we agreed upon certain game changing decisions. First of all, Incredible Cricket Association has decided to appoint my wife, Anjana Chatterjee Singh as its next chairperson and she will take charge of the office from now itself. I request the honorable treasurer Mr. Yadav to present her a bouquet of exotic flowers."

Mr. Yadav stood up to present the bouquet but could not find it anywhere on the table. Even before he could ask for it from his neighboring officials, Anjana stood up and waved in response to the thunderous cheer from the gathering.

"Where is the bouquet?" one of the officials asked the old gardener cum assistant who was standing next to the conference table.

"No bouquet has been arranged. If required, I can bring some red roses from the garden," he replied.

"No issues. Bouquet is not a necessity. Today is Valentine's Day and I will get her a tub full of roses later," said Hargurjeet and then he informed everyone that Anjana would continue the press conference.

"Thank you Mr. Yadav for such beautiful flowers. I like their smell too," with an enticing smile on her round face, she began to read her speech straight from her 8inch monster display smartphone. Perhaps that speech was the one that they worked so hard on in the extra twenty minutes of the board meeting. Some of the journalists just looked at each other but preferred not to react. They were probably interested in the dazzling beauty of Anjana and wanted her to continue speaking despite some of her irrelevant and funny words.

"After a lot of concussion, we have decided to…"

"Not concussion, it is discussion," and she was corrected by her husband, who forcefully snatched the monster display smartphone from her and increased the font size from small to large so that she could read it clearly even without her glasses.

"After a lot of discussion," she continued reading with confidence, "we have decided to increase the number of teams participating in our annual tournament from eight to sixteen. This we believe is not only a good opportunity for many new and upcoming players, but also for several new sponsors. We will have a knock out format for the 2020 edition and if things go well, that is how it would be in the future too. We have also decided to honor the most outstanding player of the tournament with The Pride of t20 cricket trophy that will comprise of a prize of rupees ten lakhs along with a gold plated miniature stump."

The positive move was appreciated by everyone and especially by Canada Singh as the increase in the number of teams gave him some hope for his own future. Zorawar, Hemant and a couple of other phenomenal players who were present for the occasion had already began to imagine themselves collecting the miniature gold plated stump along with the t20 championship trophy.

She carried on, "As you all know, there were a couple of controversies associated with the 2019 edition. In order to resolve the eve teasing issue, we have unanimously agreed to completely scrap off the post match parties and the concept of cheerleading from all matches till the end of semifinals. Though we believe cheerleaders are magnetic crowd pullers, we will have them only for the final, and this time they will be arranged by the respected Hargurjeet instead of the team owners themselves." Her reference was to the inhuman attempts made by certain team owners to woo their own cheerleaders at the post match parties.

Not all secret admirers in the gathering were impressed by the regrettable but probably wise decision. Nevertheless, they were there to report what was being said and not their own opinions and therefore all they could do was to keep their mouths shut. When the pressure increases to an unmanageable degree, even a pressure cooker needs a whistle or two to release it. Canada too needed a vent but all he found was an average sized glass of water and gulped the entire liquid in just one sip. He had never done this all his life but he was involuntarily shaking both his legs, just like some naughty kids at school do it on purpose to irritate their affectionate friends.

Adjusting the slipping pallu of her saree, Anjana continued casually towards the most awaited part of her authoritative speech, "We believe in prioritizing fair play above every other issue. A committee was formed under the leadership of our honorable board member Mr. Pradyuman Tyagi to investigate the suspicious case of the controversial coach Mr. Cunth Dhaar Singh."

The moment she mentioned his real name, anxiety sat like a fluffy snow white pillow over Canada's vacuously open maroon lipped mouth and his wedge shaped nose. Enough air could get in through it to keep his body functioning but simultaneously crippling to some extent. A couple of fresh drops of sweat appeared on his furrowed forehead despite the fact that he was sitting closest to the fan that was directed straight at him. Obviously, that fan stood there like a metallic pillar as its plug was not connected to any of the sockets. There were none near it, anyway.

"No clear evidences were found against the dubious coach during our competent internal inquiry and analytical investigation. We failed to find substantial truth in the serious allegations laid by one of our senior most umpires, Master Shams-ud-din. But, this does not necessarily mean that Mr. CD Singh is innocent. As per the memorandum of our association, without any proof of unfair play, we cannot ban him from coaching any of the existing or new teams. Instead, we would advise all team owners not to hire him as the coach of your team for the 2020 edition. Keeping in mind the fair play policy, all the current contracted players of Kanpur are instructed not to keep any kind of contact with Mr. Singh till the end of the 2020 edition of the tournament. The team owners of the Southern Blasters have submitted us a copy of the letter that clearly states that they have already fired Mr. CD Singh. And with the hope to see all of you soon for the inauguration ceremony, I conclude this formal press conference."

Some journalists quickly turned towards Canada to note his reaction, but he was nowhere to be seen. At the end of her speech, Anjana's pallu completely slipped off her shoulders but she corrected it within a few seconds. Realizing that almost everyone was busy looking at her, Canada probably left the venue as fast he could in that momentary time period.

The dejection on the face of Zorawar however was peculiarly agonizing. He was certainly one most skillful batsman ever coached by Canada. After training regularly for seven years under his beloved mentor, he had just been instructed not to contact him by any means for at least a few months. Even the pride of winning the gold plated miniature stump would leave certain part of his soul unsatisfied in the absence of his coach, he thought. But that was not it.

He had planned to tell Canada about his three year old romantic relationship with the latter's exquisitely beautiful daughter, Shefali. "What will a thirty year old like me do with that little stump in my hand when there is no Shefali in my arms!" he sighed on his way out of the farm, staring straight at the fading major lines of his right palm on the Valentine's Day noon. They were fading due to regular long hours of batting, obviously.

3

PASSIONATE LOVE IS IN THE AIR

Tuesday, 17/March/2020

It was only 9PM but the Tuesday encouraged an ominous silence to take over the locality earlier than expected. A black colored sturdy four wheel drive SUV reached the end of the lane with a non-functioning fountain of water between the walls indicating a dead end. Towards the right was an extraordinarily appealing two storey house. Though it was not as huge as some of its neighboring villas, this one was unique. It had a fairly large cricket bat made of concrete at the corner of its roof, opposite to a giant sized cement ball. Those emblems served as obvious indicators even to unsuspecting strangers that the house belonged to Canada Singh.

Dressed in a tucked out white shirt over worn out denims, Zorawar got down from his SUV but did not enter the house of his ex-mentor through its heavy iron gate. Instead, he climbed up the six feet boundary wall and jumped in, making sure not to land on the white car that was parked in the vacant space between the wall and the actual house. Like any unconscionable thief would, he then used the long and thick water pipeline to mount and reached the first floor balcony. The captain of the Southern Blasters gently knocked thrice on the lone window that was present there.

The window opened with an unexpected jerk and the wood crashed into the visitor's forehead, almost pushing him down but somehow he managed to hold on to the grill. Even if he had slipped into concussion due to the savage impact, the sparkle in the brown eyes of his girlfriend Shefali, the one who opened the window, would have brought him back to normal. "Jump in," she said in an immodest voice and that was not at all a signal of her genes, at least from the father's side.

Zorawar entered her small sized room that had pink walls. She had already locked the door for extra security. Her black hair were long and loose, obscuring the open back of her new dress, yet allowing glimpses of honeyed skin beneath. Though she wore a simple black outfit, she was a mistress at carrying almost everything with elegance. Then, she turned. Her smile created slight dimples and her eyes locked with her man's.

"I have missed you a lot. I think I know what I am supposed to do with you today," he said as she blushed.

Perhaps a lot of words were not what they wanted to exchange at that moment. They were anyway used to speaking to one another for hours every day over the phone. The dry sound made by her bracelets rubbing against each other was the only sound audible in the room as the two passionate lovers moved closer to each other. Though both had been tired and sore after a busy day, they did not care. Shefali wanted his weight on top of her so that she could squeeze him further and further but that was not how it started.

Pushing him flat on the comfortable bed, she got on top of him, something that she had never done before. She was excited as she was in the process of inventing something new, something really naughty. The diva was in complete charge as she began to unbutton his white shirt, revealing the scattered black hair of his chest, followed by his six pack abs.

As she was about to tightly grip the pillow at the back of his head in her fists, there was a knock at the door. "A daughter like you is the cause of my high blood pressure," screamed Silky, Shefali's enraged mother, in her loud husky voice. She was exactly behind the locked door.

Zorawar had already grasped his electrified girl by her perversely slender waist. Due to the sudden screams, she lost both her grip and her balance. She fell with her chin striking the pillow and her fevered mammary glands hitting him right across his face. Obviously, without complaining at all about the collision, he was quick to release her and jump out of the window as she ran to open the door.

Silky had already changed to her white maxi with floral pattern. Not only did she have an accelerated heart rate, but also a clenched jaw and a dry mouth. "Why did you lock the room?" she lashed out at Shefali. The father's princess probably had increased tension in the muscles of her limbs and some butterflies in her stomach as she could not answer her mother until she asked the same question again. Shaking her delicately waxed legs, she answered, "I was changing," and then wrapped her arms around herself.

"Where is your night suit?" Her mother shouted at the top of her voice.

Shefali looked around with wide eyes realizing that she had forgot to carry it from the drawing room when she was on her way to her room after dinner.

"Here it is," said Silky as she threw the purple colored night suit next to the pillow on the bed and left the room. The fact that her mother had no clue about her boyfriend's visit calmed her down and she took a sigh of relief.

Meanwhile, Zorawar descended to the ground floor using the pipeline. A sensual moment with Shefali had made him hard and that made it difficult for him to walk straight for a minute or so. Closing his buttons and taking some weird steps towards the wall, he somehow managed to jump over it and reach his SUV. Just as he was looking for the keys in the pocket of his jeans, he felt a rather heavy hand at his shoulder. It was Canada who had spotted his former player from the back. Not knowing what to do, Zorawar froze at the spot where he was standing with goose bumps on his hands.

"Zorawar, my boy, what are you doing here?" said the coach, surprisingly not like a formal mentor, but like a person who shared a bond of mutual affection with his players.

"Sir I had come to meet my good friend and your neighbor, Gunjan Sharma," he said in his regular tone. Despite his best try, his body language meandered within the thin line between complete diffidence and minimum confidence.

"But tomorrow is her wedding, she might be busy."

"Yes, the rituals are keeping her tremendously busy. I came to convey my best wishes to her," he said lowering his eyes towards the handle of the door of his SUV.

"Strange that she is still in Kanpur despite her destination wedding in Goa," Canada turned towards the Sharma villa to observe the lights there, only to find that all of them were switched off.

"You are correct. I had come to wish her but realized that she is not in town. I will wish her later over the phone," Zorawar replied looking with an open mouth towards the bright lights of the Jamal villa thinking it was Sharma villa.

"No issues Zorawar. Look here, I have just bought a quarter of your favorite brand of whiskey, come inside and join me for a peg," Canada said pointing towards the box containing the expensive bottle.

Zorawar desperately wanted a drink. He had half of a quarter and a water bottle in the dashboard of his SUV and could not wait to get his hands to it. Somehow he controlled his craving and politely said, "Sir, contracted players like me have been banned from keeping contact with you till the end of this year's tournament. I would love to join you but if someone sees me with you, I will not be able to participate in the mega event."

Nodding his head like a kid at pre-school, Canada said, "Go from here my boy, this place is full of eyes on all sides," and then turned his eyes towards the Jamals' window till he was satisfied that nobody was spying from there.

Zorawar unlocked his car and sat on the driver's seat. Just before closing the door, he said, "Sir, teams have been advised not to hire you as their coach but there is no restriction on you to buy, create, manage and coach your own team. Perhaps the only obstacle in your path would be that none of the contracted players would play for you. Still, I request you to consider it because Incredible Cricket Championship without you will be as boring as watching grass grow."

And then Zorawar drove away, leaving his coach speechless and totally motionless for a moment just outside the gate of his own house. Unless a person trains himself in critical thought, he would always be a comical puppet of others. "You are attractive as a magnet, you are deep as a sea, you are the defeater of the waves, you are the rescuer of the storm, you are the one and the only Cunth Dhaar," Canada remembered the words of his late father. "It is not bad to learn from the younger lot and perhaps Zorawar just pointed out the exact thing I need to do," he murmured as he walked in through the gate.

The window at the balcony of the first floor was still open and Canada spotted it in no time. Standing next to his car, he shouted, "Shefali, my darling daughter," in a loop till she appeared on the balcony with a face, red in anger or perhaps annoyance. "What is wrong with you dad, why are you also shouting at me so much?"

"My princess, the pollution levels are sky high. I request you to close the window," he said, realizing that an unnecessary fight between the mother and daughter had just taken place inside. Shefali closed the window in frustration making a noise loud enough for Jamal aunty to peep out of her window. Canada was quick to wave his hands to Mrs. Jamal and that irritated her so much that she closed her window so hard that it gave an echo effect to the previous noise.

4

THE HONORABLE BUT DIFFICULT DECISION

Monday, 04/May/2020

As the clock struck twelve, Canada entered the poorly lit and non-air-conditioned office of a creditable cumin seed exporter. If there ever was a quiz related to the names of companies, there would never be any brownie points rewarded to guess the name of this one. It was indeed Gupta Exports. "Who other than a self proclaimed wise Baniya can run a cumin seed business," thought Canada as he walked towards the grey haired receptionist cum data entry operator. There were limited options for him anyway because there was no other staff member in the entire office.

"I am Canada Singh and I wish to meet your boss for a sponsorship opportunity," he said enthusiastically.

The receptionist requested him to wait. Walking faster than most females of her age group, she went inside her boss Mr. Gupta's cabin to inform him about the Sikh guest.

"These Punjabis show off a lot Phulan aunty. They take loans, drive the most high priced luxury cars and purposely get those windshields blinded. So much pain only to hide the name of the local brand of whiskey they consume inside their car. This guy is probably here to trick me with his friendly talks and then loot some of my hard earned money. By the way, in which car did he arrive?" asked Mr. Gupta, erecting his spine after laboring for some hours on his vintage box screened computer.

"I am not sure about the model of the car but he has come in a cab."

"Oh! We have a Punjabi not showing off. This means he is already rich. We cannot waste our money on the rich. Tell him that Mr. Gupta is not interested in any sponsorship," and he chuckled in a manner similar to that of a girl whose boyfriend had just shaved his beard after months.

The receptionist returned with a blank face and said, "Sir is not interested in any sponsorship. You may leave."

"Oh tell these Baniyas to join the army first and then blabber what they want to against Punjabis." Perhaps Canada had heard Mr. Gupta's remarks and for a moment he forgot that the time as well as the place was against him. It was evident first in his eyes, then a tension of his muscles but he did not lose the ability to think clearly. He stopped his speech midway and simply walked out of there, towards the fine dine restaurant nearby to try his luck.

"No sir, our boss, Ms. Toasty Chopra is not here as of now. If you can wait for half an hour or so, I think you will be able to meet her," said the manager of the restaurant who was yet to wear his pink blazer over his black shirt.

"Yes, I will wait. I am too hungry. Show me the menu," replied Canada as he sat on the grey sofa which also had a tinge of mauve. The ethereal thought of tasty food had already calmed him down after the senseless encounter at Gupta Exports.

The menu was something that Canada had not expected it to be like. He had been to various food cafes in various cities in the past, but never had he opted to order 'Olive oil drizzled Bruschetta', never. And he ordered it not because it was the only dish below four hundred bucks, but because its name had the easiest pronunciation among all others mentioned in the menu. "Easy to order might be delicious to eat too," he said to himself.

Toasty, a confident twenty seven year old food entrepreneur, arrived before the Bruschetta and sat opposite to her guest for the meeting. Her courteous smile added charm to her angelic beauty.

"I am Canada Singh, the cricket coach you may have heard of and I am here to talk to you regarding sponsorship for my new team."

"Who has not heard of you? I do read newspapers and follow the local news too. Have your Bruschetta and leave my place you cheat." Though her nail art was pretty and her voice melodious, she sounded as arrogant as a fool and as rude as an experienced peon in a Government office, both at the same time.

It took a couple of seconds for Canada to digest her reaction but she did not wait for it. Before he could say anything, she stood up and left. Judging by the superficial smile which she still sported at the billing desk, it was evident that she did not want to create a scene at her workplace. Though the coach wanted to utter some of the most vindictive Punjabi words, he somehow controlled his feelings from leaking out and maintained absolute silence.

The waiter came smiling with a tray and said, "Here is your Olive oil drizzled Bruschetta Sir. Enjoy your meal and be careful as the plate is hot!"

The Bruschetta was indeed hot. It cost Canada around six hundred after adding the taxes, service charge and also the money he spent on the corner cart's *Chola Kulcha* after exiting the fine dine restaurant. But, he did not mind it much as it opened his eyes.

Canada did not have the habit of giving up so easily. Despite his sinking confidence, he tried out his luck with a couple of other potential sponsors but the result was no different. He felt lost, confused and uncertain, all at the same time but years of experience prevented him from getting outraged. He was like a ball of tangled yarn. The parts that were tangled were available, useable; the rest a mess, useless until united.

That mess was not going to end anytime soon and he realized that probably all his attempts to get any sponsor for his team were going to be unyielding. No doubt that he had a good marketing opportunity for the sponsors but what he lacked was a good reputation. He had had enough to realize that they would simply not trust him because of his wretched and grim history.

Canada sat motionless on the maroon threadbare sofa of his living room with a glass of whiskey to console him as his wife was busy preparing the dinner for all three of them. His shoulders appeared to be pulled by an increased force of gravity and his eyes were cast down in a blank yet mournful gaze.

"Silky," he said to his wife as he started consuming the first peg of whiskey just before dinner, "I have realized that nobody is going to sponsor my team. They still believe that I cheated that day." The pitch of his voice was as low as that of a warm hearted doctor informing about an infectious disease to his nervous patient.

"What a nincompoop am I married to? Whole day, whole night this man is talking about cricket and coaching. And now he has become mad over sponsorship. Oh God, please save me from this torment," replied Silky, who had already changed to her favorite white maxi with a floral pattern.

"Thapp," was the sound made by a steel spoon as it fell off her hands while trying to taste the dish she had just cooked.

"Now eat the potato without salt. I am not going to adjust its volume again and again," she continued to fume.

It was good that there was no guest at the home that day otherwise the mortifying tone which Silky used for her reply would have just left Canada red faced and at total loss of words. On the other hand, humiliation in front of his loving daughter was something he was used to.

"Dad, do not worry about them, I am with you," said the gorgeous Shefali who proceeded towards giving her dejected father a solemn hug.

"This girl thinks that her mother is a 24 hour working maid. Do you know I had a caesarian-section to bring you to earth? I will not keep that garish lipstick back into the makeup box. How does it bother me? Let everything remain scattered, let the house look as dirty as you can," shouted Silky from the kitchen, proving that mothers keep an eye on their children no matter where they are and what the situation is. Shefali realized her mistake and instead of hugging her father, she opted to keep back the lipstick where it belonged.

With the explosive mood that Silky was in, both Canada and Shefali realized that it was not only convenient but also wiser to talk at the dinner table. Perhaps they were used to such a treatment.

"That means the entire sum of ten lakh rupees which you have spent to buy a non-existing team is going to go into the garbage. Have you gone mad?" exclaimed Silky as her husband just said that he would go ahead into the tournament without any sponsor for his team.

"Yes. I have gone mad since the time I was wrongly blamed for the loss of my team," his voice gained loudness and momentum as he spoke his heart out.

"Do you know a single player who would play for you? In order to pay the players, will you even sell the jewels my mother presented to me at the time of our wedding?" shouted Silky with her widely open eyes revealing the anger that had boiled up inside her, not only because of her husband's monumentally foolish decision, but also because of less salt in the potato.

"Ten lakhs is the amount I have deposited by breaking my own fixed deposit to get my team registered for the tournament. Apart from that, I will have to pay twenty thousand per player to play for me. We can have a minimum of thirteen players, so that makes it around two lakh sixty thousand. Luckily, there are no cheerleaders this time. The player hunting, advertisement, equipment, jerseys and ground bookings for practice sessions would cost around a lakh and a half. The medical staff is optional, so I have decided not to go for them," explained Canada without breaking the flow of his speech even once. It was quite evident that he had already made a decision and being a diehard fan of a brother like Bollywood actor, he would obviously not listen even to himself after committing.

"Overall an amount of fourteen lakhs will be spent by you?" said Shefali as she hurriedly took a bite of her last Roti. She was visibly nervous.

"If we win the tournament, we get twenty lakhs and if we are runners up, we get fifteen lakhs."

"The potato I just cooked was not just salt less but tasteless too. This gone case man has eaten it without realizing it. And now he will waste fourteen lakhs without realizing that he has a young daughter who would get married soon. God save me from such brainless people," said Silky carrying the pile of used plates towards the kitchen.

"Dad, I know what you feel about this tournament. I also know how desperate you are for this trophy. I know you want to prove a point to every person. What I don't know is how you would create a team from scratch for this unreal endeavor." Shefali probably wanted to blindly support her father but was somewhat confused because of her mother's anger.

"Character of a man cannot be developed if he walks only on a path covered with soft, satin covered cushions. Experience has strengthened my soul and self-confidence has inspired my ambition. Whether I will achieve success or no, I cannot say now but one thing that I can assure you is that I will not leave any stone unturned to achieve my goal." His body language did not show that he had ever known failure in his life. Everything from the way he held himself, to the way he spoke, to that look of unassailable confidence in his eye said that he could do it.

Silky returned. She had heard each and every word. Now that the kitchen work was over, she was back to being normal. She said, "What else can we do but to believe you? Invest fourteen and I am sure we will get back fifteen if not twenty. Shefali, I promise to buy you the camera you so badly need for your fashion blog with the extra lakh."

"We believe in you dad, scrap some bucks off because my friends and I would get the jerseys for the players of your team for free!"

The first hug that Canada received was from his princess. The cuddle felt like a little touch of heaven, a symbol of togetherness, a deep, unbreakable, perhaps even telepathic bond between the father and his daughter. The scene reminded Silky of the moment from the past when the little Shefali used to sleep in her dad's arms. Though big enough to be a baby, she was still young, very young. For more than ten minutes, she kept her head buried into the woolen jacket of her father, perhaps to hear her own name deep within his heart and that too in a loop. Meanwhile, her mother tapped over her forehead in the way she used to over two decades ago. Silky and Canada exchanged constant eye contact but chose not to speak anything.

5

THE MOST AWAITED RETURN OF MONTY C DHINGRA

Sunday, 17/May/2020

At Monty's 1BHK flat

Rita was quick to arrange the newspaper and a bowl containing twelve boiled eggs for her chief's breakfast. Dressed in a plain Irish green t-shirt and a navy blue jogger, Monty glanced at the black and flashy tuxedo that hung desirably in the all-purpose wardrobe. Perhaps it sung some of the most thrilling tales of his treasured memories and also the hopes he had for his distant future. Apart from gaining at least 10kilograms in the last few months due to lack of physical activities, he had also changed his hairstyle to the one sported by a famous footballer. Some may compare his sheer inactivity to the laziness of a sloth but the fact was that just for a change he had purposely grown his beard thick and full, similar to that of a well known Bollywood villain.

He walked quietly towards his white plastic chair at the pace of a tortoise, albeit with the facial expression of a hunted lion, the one who is down but not out. Taking in the first bite, he simultaneously began to read the newspaper. The private investigator had no interest in reading the front page headlines as he already knew in detail about every major piece of news from the previous day. Turning the page before he could even complete the first egg, he started reading the local news and the classifieds.

One of the headings stated, 'Golden Nanavati arrested during haircut; was a wanted jewel thief.' But that was not it. The main line was the one that followed. 'The barber on duty set to protest and lodge a complaint against the police as he was not paid for his service. The police entered his shop, brushed him aside and took away his client with them.' Though the barber sounded logical, thought Monty, Mr. Nanavati's hideous photograph in which he was showing his yellowish teeth and happily flaunting his half bald, half haired look, could have been avoided by the editors.

The other news headline read, 'Boy who failed in all subjects at high school credits his girlfriend's video calls for the achievement.' These were the type of news that helped the pristine lips make an upward curve even during the rest days.

And then as he flipped some more pages till the two gemstones of Onyx froze at a half page black and white ad on the sports page. It read, 'Award winning cricket coach Canada Singh is looking for young and raw talent for his unnamed team that will participate in Kanpur's most prestigious tournament,

Incredible Cricket Championship, 2020. Interested individuals are requested to reach Shakuni Children's Park on Tuesday, 19th of May, 2020 latest by 11AM for trials and selection. No meals would be provided and participants are also requested to carry their own water bottles.' And it was followed by the obligatory mobile number for the people who always need some extra details.

Monty had found inner peace after several months of rehabilitation post his ten day imprisonment. His disreputable addiction had been conquered and it was the right time now for him to feel some happiness. And what bigger joy than to play a delightful sport that he loved so much. Though he had not played much cricket for almost a decade, just a thought of it instilled excitement in his recuperating soul. He could already imagine himself batting in a tricky situation during a tough encounter.

"Hello Sir, this is Monty C Dhingra this side and would love to join your team!" He wasted no time in calling, not for the extra details but for confirmation.

"Oh! Are you the popular investigator Monty?" replied a familiar crisp voice.

"Yes Canada Sir. I am your student who opted for investigation as a profession. Hope you have been good. Several years have gone by but it feels that it was just yesterday when I heard your manly voice!"

"Monty, my boy, come to Shakuni Children's Park on Monday. You need some practice before the tournament begins!"

"Sir, do your words mean that I am already selected?"

"My boy I have a big task ahead of me. I have coached you for a couple of years during your college days and I am completely aware of the talent you possess. If I can get you back into form with some useful tips and a lot of practice, you will be an asset for my team of amateurs."

"I will be there sir! Let us get the combination right and aim for the trophy!"

"Cheers!"

There was an explosion in Monty's brain. It was a good one, the one that carries more possibilities than he could be conscious of. There were tens of ideas there in that buzz of electricity and he could feel each of them individually. It was the invitation to a mighty adventure, to unexplored paths awaiting his feet. Whatever was ahead could be a great challenge. He was thoroughly aware that there could also be some niggles and tears but it was his experience to take and so he smiled.

"Rita, you just earned a holiday on Tuesday," he exclaimed and then gulped down the remaining eggs like a starving individual who finally gets something to eat when the aid arrives.

"I told you I have invited a couple of sisters here on Tuesday as there is no place to accommodate them for a get together at my home!" shouted Rita in a discourteous tone that was enough to suggest that she was not going to take a holiday on Tuesday.

"I won't be here. Change the venue!"

"All bosses are like that. They have no human values."

"But I value my employees."

"This month my salary ascertained that what you just said is a colossal lie."

And then there was a verbal but not emotional silence as Monty took measured steps towards his bedroom with unusually serious yet compassionate facial expressions. Entering through the door, he paused momentarily to say, "Call them here, have fun but not inside my bedroom."

Rita was obviously delighted. Perhaps she was a rare commodity - an employee who did not want a holiday; if inviting cousins for a get together at the workplace is not considered as one.

6

IMPARTIAL TRIALS

Tuesday, 19/May/2020

The radiant morning brought with it more elation than ever in the part of Shefali that peeked inside furtively through the gate of Shakuni Children's Park. Her best friends from college, a girl with a short, boyish haircut, Tara and a boy with long, girlish haircut, Tanmey were already at the venue to help her and her father with smooth conduction of the remarkable and somewhat incomprehensible event. Tara was also the owner of an online stationery shop and to aid her uncle, she gifted him a blue gel pen and a brand new spiral notebook which had a cricket bat vividly illustrated on its cover.

"We are your active assistants for the day uncle," said Tanmey as he bent over to touch Canada's feet. Tara took the kit bag containing the stumps, batting gloves, a couple of heavy bats and a dozen balls which Canada had carried with him for the trials, and placed it on the ground.

"Thank you my lovely kids! When the boys begin to come, Tara will help them fill in the registration forms and Tanmey will make them sit in order till the game begins. I have already explained to Shefali, the entire procedure to be followed during today's trials. You three can discuss among yourselves as to how to go about it. Meanwhile, all four of us can jointly erect the practice net on the corner pitch." Canada sounded optimistic of hunting some quality raw talent for his new team.

Hardly had the net been erected, there came a couple of teenage boys for the trials and as planned, Tara, Tanmey and Shefali took their positions for a serene registration process. They kept coming, one or two at a time till there were forty seven of them by the deadline and that satisfied Canada. After all years of honest hard work, sincere dedication and unselfish commitment cannot be made insignificant by one unreliable man's words.

Though most of the boys were well behaved, Tanmey wastefully struggled to make them maintain pin drop silence. As the coach was busy jotting down some vital points on the second page of his new spiral notebook, there ran in two similar looking youthful lads with the shorter one carrying a worn-out cricket bat in his left hand.

"We apologize for being late. We came straight from IIT on a bicycle with punctured rear tyre," said the taller bloke sounding as hoarse as a crow in the evening.

"So you are both students from IIT?" questioned Tara.

"No, we stay near the IIT campus. We are real brothers."

"Hey brother, what in this world is a fake brother?" the coach was perhaps still frustrated with the decorum of the previous bunch of contestants as he replied without looking towards the new entrants.

"The strangers we see on the road side and they say, Bro move aside, let me pass," the shorter one replied within a second and then he coughed twice.

The coach raised his head a little to take a look at the gangling physique of both the boys. The tall lad appeared a shade browner than the short one but you never know which child gets which traits from which parent. The only thing similar between them was their innocent looking babyish face.

"What are your names and what do you specialize in?"

"I am Alpha Kumar and I am a left hand batsman and a slow left hand orthodox bowler. He is Beta Kumar, my younger brother, a right arm swing bowler and right hand explosive batsman," said Alpha in a tone that assured the coach that these boys had practiced this dialog for at least an hour.

"You guys sound positive and appear tough. Fill in the form and join the other guys to my left. We would begin with the trials in the next five minutes," said the coach pointing towards the rest of the boys who were sitting in a squatting position with their jovial faces full of excitement.

Although it was just 11AM but the manner in which the sun was trying to torment the earthlings could make many feel that it was well past noon. Perhaps the lack of clouds helped its cause. The patches of brown on the green grass of Shakuni Children's Park and the couple of mango trees near its gate teamed up with the clear blue sky to portray fantastic scenery, perhaps the one straight out of any accomplished artist's treasured painting. However, the multi-colored kids' swings and the two buildings on either side of the mysterious bungalow opposite to the park were a bit of distraction.

As the boys got a little impatient due to the delay in the commencement of trials, there entered a two door, grey colored Challenger creating a noxious cloud of dust right behind it. If any Bollywood director was present there, he would have surely emulated that spectacle into the scene of entry of his hero, replacing those barking street dogs with a couple of untrained, skittish horses, and those innocent looking players with a group of rumpled goons ready to fight. The door opened and out came Monty C Dhingra, shoe first and the branded shades at last. The only two things missing there were perhaps a fan to blow the hero's hair in order to generate the wind effect and some indignant background music.

They say that even when the things go horribly wrong, they do not seem wrong if you have the confidence to overpower the barriers. Monty stepped on the cow dung that lay on the ground, next to the door of his esteemed car. He knew that all eyes were directed straight at him and therefore, did not want to show any sign of diffidence, though the dung was considerably fresh and wet. Using his clenched fists to fly away the flies that had flown upwards due to the ferocious impact, he walked towards the coach with his shoulders back and chin raised up as if nothing had happened. His steps were however short because of his multiple attempts to wipe the dung off on the indescribably beautiful carpet of green grass.

"Am I late Canada Sir?" he said to his former and future mentor as he took his shades off.

"Monty! My boy! Welcome to the trials! You got to practice hard to regain that college time form!" The moment Canada said this, there were some murmurs among the other boys as the coach's words obviously meant that this new celebrity like entrant was already selected.

"I will try my best and before you say anything, I will myself clear all your serious doubts. I assure you that I will not let the aghast and uncomfortable memories of the neighborhood of this venue haunt me ever again. Not just these practice sessions, I include my entire life time when I say that."

"That's the only concern I had and thanks for clearing it," said Canada and then he turned towards the boys and changed his tone from a caring father figure to the one similar to the Maths teacher of any government school. "Each one of you has already mentioned your skills in the registration form. Tara and Shefali will send you all one by one to the practice net. Each bowler will get a minimum of one over to prove his skill and each batsman will get at least twelve balls, six from the spinners and six from the pacers to showcase their talent. The allrounders get to do both. We will not follow it up with a fielding and catching session as I believe I can train anybody and turn him into a good fielder within a month. Those of you who have brought your own equipment can play with it. Others can play with the bat and gloves I have arranged specifically for this selection. I will announce the list of selected candidates today itself."

The first batsman for the selection was the left handed Kunal Khanna, the famous thirty two year old psychological illusionist of Kanpur. If the irresistibly real excitement and the highly secret bank balance were measured using the same unit, Kunal's two measurements would indeed be at par with each other. It was an extremely poor delivery from the off spinner Taufiq to begin the trials and Kunal easily slashed it towards the offside, a shot that the best of players would be proud of, if played in a gap during any match.

There was something quirky about Canada Singh. He was as aware and attentive as a soldier on duty at the international border, but as silent as a shadow speaking to its creator. Even his facial expressions matched those of his own shadow. Perhaps he did not want to leak any of his thoughts to anybody until the entire selection process was over. His black eyeballs did not deviate more than an inch away from any of the players. They kept turning up one by one for the display of their raw but pure talent and he kept observing them with as much calm as there exists in the Milky Way outside the Earth. Not only did he notice the skill, he also noticed the body language and the different kind of nervous energy that each one of them carried with them to the net. The only action he did was to note down certain points in his spiral notebook.

The event was eminently well managed by Shefali and her two friends. In the first ninety minutes of the rigorous trials, a tall and dark guy in a torn brown t-shirt, Kalee, was the only bowler to receive an instruction from Canada to bowl three overs instead of one, despite the fact that most of his deliveries were wayward. Maybe Canada wanted to concentrate on the batsmen for a while as simultaneous attention at both ends for ninety minutes without a break was too much at fifty five.

The last batsman to walk in to the net for his trial was indeed Monty and the second last bowler was Beta Kumar, who was already high on confidence after his brilliant attacking display of batting. As the two crossed each other in the middle of the pitch, Beta unexpectedly chirped into Monty's ears, "I heard Scarlett is still alive!" followed by a loud cough due to his sore throat. Monty immediately knew what Beta was trying and instead of frustration, he responded with a faint, supercilious smile as he walked towards the stumps to take guard.

The first ball was an absolute jaffa, which could not have been pitched any better. Monty failed miserably to combat the swing and edged it. If there was a wicketkeeper instead of the wall at the back, it would have been the easiest of the catches. The next two deliveries were also in that corridor of uncertainty and Monty struggled to even put bat to ball. Beta got the yorker spot on in his fourth attempt, and Monty had no answers. The ball slipped into his defense and clattered into the leg stump. Even the fifth and the sixth balls tricked the batsman into playing shots which could barely make the ball go pass the bowler himself. Monty kept the smile intact despite the maiden and multiple wickets over. "Scarlett is still alive!" repeated Beta, looking straight into the face of the batsman as he passed the ball to his brother Alpha Kumar, who was ready to bowl some left arm spin. He was accurate too and though he could not break the stumps, he had Monty defending or missing each of his six deliveries.

"And this concludes the trials! Sir will now announce his new team," said Tanmey who had been watching the game closely but perhaps was immensely confident of his own skills and therefore decided not to put himself into the selection process. Based on their own performance, some of the players were severely disappointed as they already knew their fate, while some were still hopeful. A few of them including Beta, Kunal and Mahesh were confident of making it through.

"I thank each one of you for turning up today and giving it your best shot to be a part of a team which is going to be the only amateur team of the tournament and will compete against the strongest professional cricketers of Kanpur within a month. The selected players are instructed to be present on Saturday morning at this very venue for the first practice session. Using all my experience and observation, I have selected the following players. The batsmen include Kunal Khanna, Mohammad Junaid, Sarfaraz, Dipshit Dixit and Monty C Dhingra. The allrounders are Beta Kumar, Alpha Kumar and Kamlesh Tiwari. The bowlers selected are Pappu Yadav, Jaganbir Arora, Ratandeep Lamba and Kalee. There is still one place left in the thirteen man team and that is for the wicketkeeper. Unfortunately, not a single keeper turned up today but I will make sure to find one soon for my new team."

The announcement was followed by a lot of unreasoned disappointment on many faces. Some of the shoulders slumped and the contemplative eyes cast down in mournful gaze, some even tried to kick the little stones that lay here and there on their way to the exit. Not everyone has the capability to accept rejection with grace. There always are some inveterate rebels.

"This man is a cheat and his team will lose badly! Mark my words," shouted Mahesh who was not selected despite his fine batting display. He was loud enough, perhaps on purpose to make sure that Canada hears those pinching words. "This is a team of losers! He chose that drug addict Monty over me! One can easily understand their standard," added another rejected batsman on his way out of the park. "The old man has gone mad. He picked Kalee who cannot even bowl a couple of proper deliveries in one over. What a time waste this event has been on a Tuesday!" said Taufiq who had taken a leave from his bank in order to try his luck. The coach had expected this and was thoroughly prepared. He did not react a bit and maintained his poker face as it was during the game. Luckily, there were no physically violent ones in the group.

On the other hand, for the twelve players selected it was a moment to cherish. The sublime happiness on their faces was similar to the one on the studious face of the topper after the examination results are declared. Kunal even jumped to congratulate his new teammates as all of them shook hands with each other. Perhaps Monty and Beta were the only two who did not congratulate one another.

"Welcome to the family! We will decide the name of the team within a couple of days and I will formally submit the list containing the players name to the organizers tomorrow itself. Each one of you would be paid twenty thousand for playing for my team. The official letters of selection will be provided soon. I also would instruct all of you that though you are excited, you need to be smart too. I have the responsibility of training you all not just to compete, but win the Incredible Cricket Championship 2020, but at the same time you all have the responsibility of being serious and try hard to win all our matches."

"Yes Sir, we will!" said the excited lot as they made their way out of the park, talking to each other, perhaps introducing themselves to their new buddies before the formal team meeting.

Monty was the only one who stayed back. He said to his coach, "Sir, I think I know a guy who can be the wicketkeeper for our team."

"Who is he?"

"I still remember the usefully vague term he used last year when I met him. He said that his jump was so long and cold that even the eight feet kangaroos of Australia would be ashamed when they see the unscheduled and asymmetric jump of an Indian man. Though almost touching forty, he is physically quite fit and mentally stable to handle pressure situations. He could jump and catch his employer Scarlett White whenever the need arose and I am sure he can catch the ball well behind the stumps too. He is a cab driver by profession but not an ordinary one by any stretch of imagination. His name is Sooraj Singh. I still have his mobile number and if you say, I can share it with you!"

The coach did not have a fantastically wide choice. He agreed to invite the proposed man but fifteen minutes earlier than the other selected players so that the little trial session does not hamper the first team practice session.

"Sir, if you do not mind, who are these three assisting you?"

"She is my daughter Shefali and these are her friends, Tanmey and Tara."

Tara was waiting for this moment. She had been observing Monty for a long time, perhaps from the moment he made his entry in Challenger. Love at first sight is not really what she believed in but the extremely magnetic personality of Monty had successfully changed that thought process of many in the past too. She was single after all and considered her short hair a sort of a disadvantage when it came to wooing the out of ordinary men. As the two gemstones of Onyx turned towards her, she blushed vividly. There was a sudden increase in the level of some particular hormones in her body. She did not know which ones but certainly they were the electrostatic ones that act as chemical messengers in the brain.

"Nice hairstyle you have Tara! Something quite different from most of the girls," said Monty. Physically she was standing there but Tara's mind seemed to have gone on a sultry long vacation. By the time she responded with a thank you, Monty had already completed warm handshakes with Shefali and Tanmey and was on his way to his Challenger.

"He still has it in him!" said Canada admiring the charm of his team's batsman as he silently observed the change in Tara's body language.

"But Sir, why did you not select Mahesh? He was batting really well," Tanmey tried to clear his doubt.

"One month is too less time period to train this bunch of laymen for their competition against some of the most highly skilled and professional cricketers. No doubt Mahesh is a good batsman, but I know that being a corporate employee, he will not be regular to the practice sessions. I have kept each aspect in my mind for this team's formulation. I cannot take any risk with it. Just hope that the proposed wicketkeeper turns out to be good."

"Fingers crossed," said Tanmey and he proceeded along with Shefali and Canada to take down the practice net, while Tara stood motionless, looking vehemently at the park's gate from where the Challenger had exited five minutes ago.

7

FIRST PRACTICE SESSION

Saturday, 23/May/2020

"**H**i," greeted Tara with an uncharacteristic mirthless smile up on her face when Beta, Alpha and Pappu entered the park together for the first practice session.

"Hello," said Pappu after thumping the narrow gut of Beta with the pointed end of his elbow. Though his intention was to set the encaged butterflies free, the gentle strike was also successful in preventing the latter from sticking his long tongue out like an Indian Pariah dog. Plainly Pappu did not want Tara to know that he and his friends had studied whole life in boys' school.

"You guys have come five minutes earlier than the designated time," she said as her smile changed to an unpleasant sunken grin.

"We are currently jobless so came here early to help you with the ponderous erection of the practice nets," responded Alpha. Not at all pleased by the response, the shortest member of the team, Pappu closed his loathsome eyes and added, "Have you seen any retro music video with our comment that reads, who is watching this in 2020? I guess no and that proves that we are not totally jobless after all.”

“She is listening to your words so carefully,” said Beta.

With a hopeful smile that was more due to absurd and unaccountable shyness than anything else, Pappu opened his eyes to see that Tara had already left the three players alone near the gate. She was standing with Tanmey, Shefali, Canada and a six feet tall man with long and bushy moustaches who appeared to have come straight out of a movie theatre’s screen that played a Bhojpuri movie.

Meanwhile, Ratandeep, Kunal, Monty and Jaganbir too came into the park, followed by Kalee, Sarfaraz, Junaid and Dipshit. “Good morning sir,” they said in unison as if Canada Singh was not a cricket coach but a school teacher being greeted by the troublesome students of his class.

“Good morning. Meet Sooraj Singh. He is the wicketkeeper of our team,” Canada introduced the mysterious man to his boys. Though Monty and Sooraj knew each other from the past, they mutually decided not to reveal their acquaintance to any other player. Beta, Alpha, Kalee and Pappu joked among themselves, “Now this uncle will keep wickets for us!” When they saw Monty staring at them like a king staring at the prisoners of war, they shut their mouths.

Tara’s face moved a little too slowly, as if she was taking in the surroundings more than anyone else. Totally engrossed in staring at Monty, she did not see a ball lying on the ground and consequently stepped over it. Though she had fallen face first on the soft, putty-like mud, Tanmey was quick to attend her. "Thank God! You did not fall on the cow dung," he said. Unfortunately, her cute pinkish full sleeved top spoiled and she was left with no other option but to go home without even watching the first practice session.

"Once upon a time, there were 200 sheep. They were instructed to reach point B from point A one by one and a fairly high wooden bench was placed at the centre of the two points to act as a hurdle," the coach began the first session with his motivational speech, "121 sheep jumped over but the 122nd one had tiny legs. Though it tried several times, it could not jump high enough to cross the gargantuan obstacle. Thinking about a method to cross the hurdle, it stood at a corner and allowed the ones behind to jump. It soon realized that there was enough empty space on both sides of the bench and took advantage of that to reach point B by just walking across like a boss."

"What is Sir trying to say?" said Alpha to Dipshit as all the other players half heartedly clapped for the intelligent sheep.

Carefully observing the reaction and body language of each of his boys, Canada continued, "We need to be like that quick witted sheep. All of us have certain limitations and we need to adjust to the situations based on the skill set we currently possess."

The claps got louder as Canada paused to drink a sip of water. Then, he said, "I will be your mentor, coach, guru, friend, strategic planner and information source. People might call us underdogs, but as the bottom of our heart would suggest, we are stubbornly brave. Therefore we are going to name our team Brave Dogs. Shefali has herself designed the logo of our team. As we are a group of unknown and infamous people, we currently have no sponsor. We do not even need them as the plain red jersey is bright enough to add more charisma to our noble personalities. Tanmey, you may distribute each Brave Dog his letter of selection and jersey."

Tanmey was quick to follow the instructions. Happiness is what the Brave Dogs felt in their heart; pride is what they decided to play for. There was emotion, gratitude, a sense of achievement, inner peace and of course excitement in every individual's face as they received their letters of selection and jerseys.

"We need to cherish this day and remember it for a long time to come. We need to keep getting scintillating performances to keep alive the faith that Canada Sir has shown in our abilities. This day marks the commencement of our cricketing journey. I can already imagine us winning the ICC 2020 trophy," said Monty as everyone except Beta heard him carefully.

Holding their red jerseys as firmly in their hands as a Bollywood heroine would hold the rope when pushed off the cliff by the villain of the movie until the hero came for her rescue. Surprisingly, after a short but animated discussion, they came up with a sentence which they decided to use as their binding anthem. With Canada's permission, each one of them shouted at the top of his voice, "You may think that we are the underdogs, but no, no, no, we are the Brave Dogs, the mighty mighty Brave Dogs! Woof, woof, woof!" Content by their excitement, Canada joined them too.

Unexpectedly, the wise and experienced coach began with the fielding drills. Perhaps that was something he always prioritized, especially for t20 cricket. "Remember we are just thirteen. Nobody will dive or jump higher than normal to stop or catch the ball. We need to be safe and use the skills that we already possess in the best way possible," said Canada angrily when Dipshit tried to dive in order to stop the ball.

Just when Beta safely took a high catch, Kamlesh came running into the park. He was visibly exhausted and running short of breath. Even the thin *choti* which always used to stay erected like an antenna over his square shaped head, had fallen downwards over his otherwise short and black hair.

"What happened," asked Tanmey as he offered a bottle of water to the thirteenth Brave Dog.

"I was coming here from Permat temple after the completion of the *pooja*. Near the fat man's ice cream rickshaw, a lady shouted, whoever wants ice cream, come and stand in the queue."

The other Brave Dogs and Canada looked at each other as if Kamlesh was a standup comedian whose jokes went radically flat.

He continued, "I stood at the thirteenth position in that queue and when my chance came, she asked me who I was. I told her my name but even before she could say a word, I realized that all others in that queue were kids from her own colony. I came running from there, hiding my face from the evil stare of the society."

"Do not laugh," said Monty to the other Brave Dogs just before they could start their laughter. He then continued with his practice of aiming and throwing the ball at the stumps from various angles and distances. Real leadership is about connecting with people and by not letting anybody mock Kamlesh for his innocence, Monty showed signs of being a good leader.

The batting and bowling practice took place simultaneously with situational fielding practice.

"Perhaps it helps playing the ball a bit later and I think Monty plays it a bit later than anybody else," remarked Canada despite the fact that Monty missed the third ball from Beta in a row.

Sooraj was amazing behind the stumps. With a lot of help from the coach and an unflinching concentration, he had already mastered the art of concurrent squatting and glove work. However, he was not up to the mark with the bat in his hand. He possessed the power and Canada knew that power would come handy when there is need to increase the run rate.

Though Kalee was all over the place and all the batsmen picked him really well, Canada seemed to be highly satisfied with his performance and wrote something in his spiral notebook.

Beta was of course the standout bowler. He had the unique talent of controlled swing with the new ball as well as some reverse swing with a slightly older ball. All Canada had to do with him was to polish his bowling action a little bit and explain him which weapon to use at which stage of the match. Also, his batting was all about power hitting, something that every team needs going into a t20 tournament.

"Master Shams-ud-din's allegations gave me a lot of motivation to not get over-excited at any stage of the match. Tell him that I will henceforth be a little more disciplined especially when he is on the ground," Canada said to Sarfaraz, who was an employee of the Master at The Powerful Horse boutique. All the young tailor did was to shake his head.

"Jaganbir, you can generate more pace if you run faster," pointed out Canada but was surprised to see the bowler's shoulders droop on hearing this.

"What is the matter?"

"I use the hair at the back of my head to cover the vacant area right above my forehead. If I run fast, the hair will fly away and the front portion of my head will be completely revealed," Jaganbir expressed his sorrow.

Canada was taken aback by the inferiority complex that his player had in his mind.

Though some players wanted to laugh out loud, Monty did not allow them to. He said, "Haircut of your choice does make you more confident but you have something that none of us have, and that is the lack of hair on your head. Be that much confident so that we can be jealous of your confidence."

When assured that nobody would laugh at him, Jaganbir ran fast and consequently generated more pace. "Daily practice will make him forget about flying hair. In the worst scenario, we will give him a good quality hair gel," discussed Monty and Canada between them.

"Hey there are a couple of missed calls on your phone," said Alpha to Pappu, who was engrossed in spinning the ball as much as he could.

"Oh! My mother is calling me," he said and called her back but there was no response from the other end. "I will call her again after sometime," he said and went to bowl another over of vicious spin to Junaid and Dipshit. When he returned, there were 32 missed calls from his mother. He called her back immediately but once again there was no response. "I think she wants to remind me to get bananas for tomorrow's breakfast," he sighed.

After practicing for around four hours, just before Canada was about to disperse the squad, he made an important announcement, "I hereby appoint Monty C Dhingra the captain of this team and Kunal will be his deputy."

Happy was a relative term for most of the Brave Dogs. They saw what exactly had made Canada take that decision, yet for the Kumar brothers the declaration was not a wise one. Beta's facial expression turned into that of a poor man whose slice of bread and shelter for the night had been snatched away from him. Though Alpha smiled, it was nothing like the one that bursts from within. Instead, it was the one being worn like an obligation. Perhaps the brothers, especially the younger one, Beta, secretly desired to be the skipper of the team. Some might even agree with his secret intentions as he was not only one of the best bowlers but also more than useful power hitter down the order.

"Maybe Sir does not want you to take carry the load of all of us on your shoulders so that you can concentrate better on your own game," whispered Alpha into his brother's ear. Though he did not register his displeasure, Beta was visibly not convinced at all.

"Remember that all of us are limited. There might be some big shots that the big players play or some big deliveries they bowl, but definitely not all of us can bat or bowl the way others do. Be limited but work out a way that works the best for our team. I will give my best and hope the same from all of you. Under the guidance of Canada sir, all of us will soon emerge as Incredible Cricket Champions!" Monty kept his first ever captain's speech as to the point as anyone possibly could.

"Before we disperse," said the vice captain Kunal, "I will show you guys a mind magic trick! I am a mentalist. I can read and influence minds. He called Ratandeep near him.

"Pick a number between 1 and 10."

"2," said the muscular six and a half feet tall Sikh player in his heavy voice.

Kunal pulled out a handkerchief from the pocket of his lower. He unfolded it to reveal that the number 2 was actually knitted on it. Thunderous claps and a lot of stunned faces was the result but Monty smiled. Probably he was the only one who had actually figured out the trick. No matter what the circumstances are, an investigator's brain is always tough to either read or influence.

"What else can you do?" asked Pappu as he rejected his mother's call for the second time in a row.

"I will show you on the ground during the match," said Kunal and the loud cheers that followed, marked the end of the laborious practice session.

8

GENTLEMEN HAVE FUN AFTER PRACTICE

Saturday, 23/May/2020

The lengthy practice session had drained most of the kinetic energy from the muscular bodies of the three newly made good friends, Monty, Kunal and Ratandeep. In order to charge up, they decided to take 600ml can of imported beer each.

"It is Saturday! Let us stroll around Swaroop Nagar for some time in this beast," said Kunal as he was quite fascinated by Monty's esteemed Challenger.

"Why just Swaroop Nagar," questioned Ratandeep as he took his seat at the back, adjacent to the Pink Teddy Bear.

"I have heard about her a lot and now I want to see that mysterious yet gorgeous girl."

"Oh the one who roams near the Chat Corner in a Punjabi suit," said Ratandeep with his lips curving slowly into a semi-pout.

"Time to re-live some bad old days," said Monty as the three players drove away into the traffic, with the Punjabi beats taking over the influence of the beer.

The desirable target did appear in a pink and yellow suit and instead of paying more attention to her beauty the three of them were more concerned with the color of her dress. While scanning her fine, soft curly, wool like hair, they did not notice that she was actually with her square built and balding boyfriend, who was staring with grotesque vision straight at them.

"Sweety, do not look towards that old model Challenger," said the boyfriend to his unaware fairy and then he walked with a lot of momentum towards the car which was parked opposite to his motorbike.

"Oh, look, Jaganbir is here," exclaimed Ratandeep as he spotted Jaganbir approaching towards their car cum bar.

"Yeah, I am here and she is mine. I humbly request you three to leave. I will give you a relaxing shoulder massage tomorrow." Jagabir's voice was as low as that of a mobile phone notification when the volume is set to its lowest limit.

"No, no, we were looking for the waiter to order our *Aloo Tikki* to help us intake this beer," Kunal was quick to respond.

Jaganbir's expressions changed as he closed his eyes momentarily, even though his girl was still standing behind his back with her head turned to another side. "But sirs, today is Saturday, the weekly off for the Chat Corner," he said. Perhaps he was embarrassed to let her know that those thirty plus single lunatics in the car, were not strangers but his own teammates.

"You have a lot of stamina Jaganbir. Look at us, we were exhausted after the practice session and here you are on a date with a..." pointed out Ratandeep, staring at his beer can but was interrupted by Monty.

"Remember this tournament will be played in the absence of cheerleaders. We need some glamour in the crowd for our moral support. See you tomorrow," said the captain as he drove the Challenger away from there, amidst oohs and aahs from his friends in the car.

"I scolded them and they ran away like cowards, let us go for a ride on my new motorbike," said Jaganbir who now acted as an angry young man with a receding hairline. She seemed happy and immediately wore the Mohawk spiked metal helmet.

"Baby, that is mine, you wear this normal helmet."

"Why?"

"I feel like I have good spiked hair when I put that on my head!"

Being an incredibly understanding girlfriend, she agreed to swap the helmets as they left the Chat Corner on the motorbike for some show off and fun.

9

TEAM OUTING RESULTS IN CHAOS

Tuesday, 07/June/2020

Seven days to go to the start of the tournament

The evening practice session that Tuesday was not just long, it was insanely tiring too. Though it lasted for almost five hours, the Brave Dogs did not complain as most of them received a lot of sincere advises and practical instructions from their ever involved coach. They even discussed certain team plans and individual roles within the squad. Despite his herculean efforts, the only thing that Canada still struggled to achieve was to inculcate into his boys a feeling of togetherness. Going into such a distinguished tournament, the presence of three distinct sub-groups within the team was a severe drawback, the one which could not be afforded under any circumstance.

As the players were busy packing their kits, Shefali in a designer black suit and Tara in a cherry red mini skirt, along with Tanmey reached the park. Tara straightaway walked up to Monty and stood still adjacent to the captain. Though Shefali did not appear much enthusiastic, she said, "Dad, we are here."

That warm feminine voice sent nerves dancing up Beta Kumar's spine. Though he was yet to keep his bat into the bag, he turned around towards his new yet passionate crush, leaving his furious elder brother Alpha to do the double packing. Normal thoughts barely formed in his innocent mind before they were replaced with the fantasies of what could be if he was brave enough to tell her. Vasectomy was a serious option after two kids with her, he discreetly thought inside his own head.

Before the rabid desire could convert into possessive conviction, Canada interrupted with his important announcement, "Today is your informal team outing, the first and the only one before the championship. Shefali, Tanmey and Tara, you three should accompany the Brave Dogs to Battlefield Café. The dinner is on me."

"You will not accompany us?" questioned Sooraj. Perhaps he was the only one who could connect really well with the age group of the coach.

"Today is dad's thirtieth wedding anniversary. He is going for a romantic dinner date with my mother and therefore cannot accompany us," informed Shefali. Though all the players right away wished Canada, Beta stood absolutely silent and motionless at one spot, bashfully smiling like the pre-contemporary but post historic newly wedded Indian brides. Perhaps the mere presence of Shefali had sent his mind into an uncontrolled, captivated spiral as if it had just branded his soul with it.

Similar was the case with Tara but at least Beta did not have to face the problem that she was in. Though she had worn that red mini skirt in order to impress Monty, it led to her hands being occupied in pulling it down again and again. Perhaps it was all right for Monty but the skin reveal was a bit too much for the unpredictable eyes of the other Brave Dogs, especially the ones from the boys' only schools.

"Battlefield is quite an old place. How about going to a newer and much happening venue?" said Tanmey, who had finished helping all the players load their kit bags in Canada's car. His volume was as low as that of a shriek of a mouse hiding in the storeroom.

"No. Go to Battlefield Café only," Canada made his point clear as he walked out of the park in haste, probably in excitement of the anticipated romance, obviously a well deserved one, after a long time.

The venue was around four kilometers from the park. Kalee and Sooraj left on the latter's bicycle, taking Pappu with them as he was thin as a pencil and somewhat narrow to sit on the frame without blocking the view of the rider. Though their sub-group members Alpha and Beta had their own bicycle, to everyone's surprise Beta said, "I can take auto with Tara and her friend. Tanmey can join Alpha on the bicycle." Though he wanted to name Shefali instead of Tara, there was something weird at the back of his mind that did not allow him to take his own crush's name.

"But I am going with Monty in his Challenger," replied Tara only to be hit on the middle of her back by Shefali and receive a puzzled look from Tanmey.

Ultimately, the three friends opted for an auto and the brothers left on their bicycle. While the elite sub-group of Monty, Ratandeep, Kunal and Jaganbir left for Battlefield Café in the Challenger, the neutrals left on their motorbikes, Sarfaraz with Junaid and Dipshit with Kamlesh.

On their way, while holding his *choti* to prevent its vertical orientation against the wind, Kamlesh simultaneously advised Dipshit to consult Kanpur's most famous saint, Kick Baba, who could actually help him do well in the tournament.

The venue chosen by Canada for the auspicious team outing was one of the oldest cafes of the town. The food was simple and the decor plain. With no background music, it was more a place for conversations than for eating. A large centre table that had been arranged for around sixteen-seventeen people was still vacant. Each sub-group of the Brave Dogs occupied their own distinct table and that too the one which was as far as possible from the other sub-group's table. Tanmey was busy changing his place from one table to other, trying really hard to coordinate the orders. Shefali and Tara obviously sat with Monty's sub-group. Each table placed a different order and was engrossed in a different conversation.

The neutrals had a mixed opinion about vegetarian and non-vegetarian options and they spent their time discussing the benefits and drawbacks of each of those options. The elites were more into the team combination and strategy building type of stuff. Though Tara wanted to talk at least something to Monty but having no idea at all about cricket did not give her an opportunity to strike any conversation with him. Having nothing else to do, she quietly sat with Shefali and forwarded not so funny memes to some of her active online groups over messages. Meanwhile, Shefali had put on a rather surprising smile across her gorgeously decorated face.

"Why is the beguiling angel sitting with those jokers," said Beta pointing towards Shefali, who was sitting exactly opposite to Monty. He was shaking his legs as violently as a man jumping on the dance on the glowing tiles game machine.

"My heart says she is not a gold digger," replied Alpha with his facial expression showing utmost concern for his younger brother.

"That means even a guy like Beta Kumar has a chance," said Pappu adding fuel to fire that was about to light.

"Yes. A girl once commented jackass on his profile picture," said Alpha closing his eyes momentarily to remember a pleasant incident from the past.

"Do you even know what jackass means?" asked Sooraj. The eldest man in the cafe had almost lost patience after sitting with a bunch of wannabes.

"It is a famous dialog of an ageless and hairy Bollywood star," replied Beta, shocked by the lack of knowledge of the wicketkeeper.

"No. It means a donkey," clarified Sooraj only to leave Beta as embarrassed as a tech blogger when someone asks her about her earnings.

"Tara's legs are very good. If only her hair was long, then it would surely have been more fun," said Kalee who had bent down to pick the spoon he just dropped on the floor for the seventh time.

"After using imported wax, I think she has polished her legs also," said Pappu who just got up after crawling with his plate which he had intentionally dropped quite far from his chair.

"When I sling a backhand slap on the left cheek, even the right one becomes red," said Sooraj who was getting irritated by the continuous espying that was going on around him.

Meanwhile, Shefali went to the washroom which was near the neutral sub-group's inattentive table.

"This is the best time, go and propose her," said Alpha handing over a slice of garlic bread from the pasta that they had ordered. Perhaps that was his unique way of proposing.

"Yeah, yeah, come on, yeah, show us the man in you," said Pappu and Kalee in chorus as if they were not players but adult performers. Surprisingly even Sooraj nodded.

Beta reached the neutral table, near the ladies' washroom in a flash with the slice of garlic bread in his left hand. "Dipshit, Kamlesh, Sarfaraz and Junaid, make the video of my proposal," he said and handed them his old model 4MP camera mobile.

"I have a better camera," said Junaid who had recently purchased a 64MP camera phone, "I will make the video from it and then message it on the team group chat."

"So, this video is going to be the first message on the group chat," said Sarfaraz, excited by Junaid's remark.

"But boys recall to your mischievous minds that Canada sir is the admin," pointed out Dipshit with a bothered look across his face.

"Share it on personal chat. Save my number," said Beta and then dictated his number to Junaid.

The washroom door opened with a weak creaky sound and out came Shefali. She had applied a fresh coat of red lipstick and perhaps even mascara.

"Action," said Kamlesh, who was the first one to take a bite of the crispy potato fries.

"I am a dry slice of bread. Will you be my butter?" said Beta looking straight through Shefali's black stilettos instead of her wide open eyes. Though he had somehow maneuvered himself into the mandatory proposal pose by getting down on his left knee, it was really difficult for him to control his nerves. He fixed the slice of garlic bread in his mouth but did not bite it. Maybe he thought that she would really spread some butter on it.

"You deserve mixed fruit jam," she replied but even before the high pitched laughter could follow, there was a gentle tap on the shoulder of Beta from behind. When he turned to look who was there, a three kilogram hand connected with his right cheek and the entire café went into a mortuary like silence for the next few seconds. The slap was so hard that the recipient slipped into momentary concussion, not just with the force of it but also its timing. Half of the slice of garlic bread fell on the floor while the other half perhaps reached somewhere deep inside his stomach without him actually tasting or biting it. However, the worst part for him was that instead of some enjoyable romance, Junaid just video recorded a fierce action sequence.

The full forced slap was indeed from Zorawar and he was probably drunk. He had just walked into the café and even before he could find a table for himself, he saw a five feet man in a soiled track pant proposing his girlfriend. Though Beta was down, his sub-group and the neutrals tried their best to put up a fight against the muscular man but retreated when they saw the entire Southern Blasters team enter the café.

The big table was obviously reserved for the Blasters. Oozing with fearless confidence, each one of them walked towards their table like they were the ruthless ancient fighters from the era of Chhatrapati Shivaji Maharaj. Their shoes made a sound similar to the clanking of swords and their body language suggested that they could even fight a howling skulk in the dark of the night and emerge victorious.

"Stop it," screamed Shefali when she spotted Zorawar proceeding to kick Beta, who was still lying on the floor like a hopeless drunkard lying in a filthy drain. Perhaps she was the only one who had the courage to speak something in that situation.

"If you look at her again with your beady eyes, it will be a no holds barred," said Zorawar bending right into the face of the fallen Brave Dog. He pulled Shefali gently towards him and she too sat with the Blasters, leaving even the elite sub-group in a shock. Even Tara and Tanmey had not expected such a scene from their best friend.

"I have heard that Canada Sir has chosen these idiots to play t20 cricket for his team at the Incredible Cricket Championship 2020," said one of the Blasters, perhaps the one who naturally had the loudest voice among all of them.

"When they are physically so weak that they cannot even stand up for a long time after just one smack, how will they compete against any other team?" said another.

"Brethren, let me show you the latest phone. Come here you cameraman," the famous fast bowler Balloo said as he called Junaid towards him.

Snatching Junaid's phone from his cold hands, the bully passed it to his mates and each one of them watched the recently recorded video of Zorawar slapping Beta. Though the video was full of jerks and unexpected noise, it seemed to entertain them until one of them permanently deleted it. The bully returned Junaid's phone saying, "Next time if you make a video featuring any of us, I will break into uncountable pieces; not only your phone but also your bones." Junaid almost had a tear in his eye for his inability to answer back.

"Hey, look at that bald boy," said one of the Blasters pointing towards Jaganbir, who was quick to turn his face away. Though he had found some confidence after Monty's words during the practice, he was not a cent percent confident yet.

"Every time he goes to wash his cartoonish face, I think his mother would shout at him for wasting both time and water," replied Balloo and his mates laughed out thunderously proving that shaming someone was their type of humor.

"What about that uncle? I think he is here to manage the other kids," they joked about Sooraj and that left the latter as red faced as an archeologist would get if someone gave him a used tampon to know which period it belonged to.

"Guys, I request you all not to pass bad comments on this team. My father has a lot of hopes that they will do well in the tournament and has not only invested lakhs of rupees but also vested hours in training and mentoring each one of them," said Shefali, who had begun to get a bit restless.

If both the teams were horses and she was a chariot, the two horses were pulling her in opposite directions. On one side was her father and she could never think to abandon the team created by him. On the other side was her boyfriend, her future. Both of them were important to her, both teams a part of her soul. The problem was that she did not know how to find a way to make both the horses charge in the same direction, to pull together.

"Which team are you supporting Shefali?" asked Zorawar who had been mute for a long time. Her lips compressed, forehead furrowed and arms crossed as if she wanted to hug herself. Obviously she had no answer. He continued, "We have maximum respect for Canada Sir. He has trained us for seven years. You can yourself see the difference in the pedigree of his past and present choices." All

Shefali could manage to do was to lower her eyes and maintain silence.

Meanwhile, one of the Blasters continued with the verbal bullying, "I have heard that their captain Monty C Dhingra is a womanizer and a drug addict. He was in jail till a few days back and now trying to play cricket. What a perfect character to lead a team of dolts!"

"You have slapped me and I haven't smacked a punch yet," said Beta. He was up on his feet and stared right into the face of Zorawar.

"You want to slap him?" said a Blaster with a comic facial expression and the others cackled.

"He will slap ten, count one," said Kunal who had lost patience due to the continuous unprovoked jeering. He moved towards the Blasters' table only to be pushed back by one of them, adding an insult to injury.

"Oh look! Rejected by each one of us, Tara is also here and that too in a mini skirt. Baby, no matter how much makeup you wear and what clothes you put on, you will look as ugly as a stinking rat with a couple of moles on its face until you get a wig made for yourself," said Balloo. Tara's face had already shrunk to a quarter of its actual size despite the fact that her mind had much more data to process.

"You have called my team a team of dolts and I haven't said a word about yours yet. You have disrespected each member of my squad and I haven't retaliated yet. Now you have crossed all limits by saying against Tara," said

Monty as he got up and gently pushed his chair below the table. Followed by Ratandeep and Kunal, he took measured steps towards the disturbing table.

Monty's words for her made Tara feel like some invisible hands just wrapped around her to make her safer. Having Monty by her side made her feel like anything was possible in the world and like she could conquer anything. She knew if it happened, Monty would be her first but what she really wished was for him to be her last.

Reaching next to Zorawar and Shefali and looking straight into the eyes of his counterpart, Monty continued, "I guarantee that unless the tournament ends, nobody from your team will get injured because of us and I expect the same guarantee from you too."

"The argument has been built to a tornado and your man is the cause," replied Zorawar referring to Beta.

"The words your boys spoke about my boys in such well intentioned purity triggered something in us. I guess they were raised that way but let me be clear, we are not that cheap. Perhaps this is the difference in the past and the present pedigree of our respected Canada Sir."

"Enough of words have been exchanged, now is the time for some action," said Pappu, the thinnest and probably even the tiniest man in the café as he threw his spoon right across the breadth of the café to land over the centre of the Blasters' table. That was a signal of the commencement of something ugly, something really filthy.

The scuffle between the players of both teams was something that was beyond Tanmey, Shefali, Tara or even the staff of the café to control. It was sort of a thirteen man tag team wrestling match, the only difference being that they did not assault each other with kicks, punches and body blows. Each player made sure that nobody from either side gets injured. Fundamentally, they were all trained by Canada Singh and true sportsmanship was the first distinctive trait he taught to each of his student.

The fight was a not a choreographed dance of destruction. It was a food wastage one with both sides throwing their dishes at each other, creating a mess all over the café. Food, cutlery and even empty cold drink bottles went flying from end to end, front to back, left to right. Spoons and folks flew across the length and the breadth of the café like the paper airplanes made by little kids at school to pass time during a boring class.

Beta passed the bowl containing tamarind chutney to Sarfaraz, who passed it to Ratandeep so even the elite table had some weapons to attack. Similarly, Jaganbir passed a dozen spoons and as many folks to Dipshit, who passed them to Kalee so that his bunker does not fall short of resources.

Unable to react to the disastrous situation, Shefali, Tara and Tanmey stood absolutely still near the exit. Perhaps that was necessary in order to save themselves from all round attack. Though she had not completely panicked, there were periodic choking sensations in Tara's throat. As one of the spoons landed near Tanmey's shoe, his heartbeat too turned a bit rapid. A couple of drops of sweat had already made their way on Shefali's broad forehead despite the fact that the air conditioner was set to the minimum possible temperature.

The powerless waiters stood like lifeless mannequins at a corner amidst the chaos as their boss had gifted them just one dress each and they could not afford multiple disheveled yellow patches on the white.

The Brave Dogs were in better position throughout the battle. Of course their presence on three different sides of the Blasters worked to their advantage. Whenever one of their tables fell short of ammunition, any other would begin double the assault while the third one passed them some resources. Whenever one of their tables was attacked more, other two were quick to guard them.

Never before had Monty's boys shown such efficient and methodical teamwork. The unnecessary fight not only managed to instill cooperation among the three sub-groups, but also a sense of unification. They also realized how important it was for a team to work as one unit.

"Put an end to this Zorawar," screamed Shefali. Though she tried her best, perhaps the growing unrestrained emotion into her head did not allow her to be as loud as she could be. Even her palms had turned completely wet in agitation. Her facial expressions clearly demonstrated that she could cry anytime if that fight did not stop soon.

Being the fierce competitor he was, Zorawar wanted to win the battle, but at the same time, he did not want to see tears in the eyes of his innocent girlfriend. Despite the fact that he was drunk, he reacted maturely. Keeping in mind the gravity of the situation, he said, "Boys, it is not worth it, let us leave. We will see them on the ground."

The moment the Blasters heard the instruction from their captain, each one of them dropped his missile. Perhaps whatever they did, they always did it together. If one abandoned something, it was compulsory for others to abandon that too. Such was the level of mutual understanding and the trust and faith they had in one another. Following Zorawar, all of them left the café, leaving it as filthy as a garbage bin that had not been cleaned for over a month. The Brave Dogs still had spoons and folks in their hands, but they unhanded them too after their opponents abruptly left the battle midway.

Kunal was quick to hug Beta. He said, "Don't worry brother. The slap on your face was a slap on the face of the Brave Dog family. We have allowed the villains to flee but I assure you that we all will take a savage revenge of the slap on the ground!"

All the thirteen players got together and formed a huddle. The captain Monty did all the talking. He said, "Sometimes it is necessary to learn from the opponents too. They came here not as fifteen individuals but as one unit. We came here in three different units which cannot be even termed as sub-units of one. The slap across Beta's face is the slap that should wake all of us up. Though we came as individuals of our sub-groups, we will leave this café as one entity – the mighty mighty Brave Dogs. Woof, woof, woof." The entire café echoed with the sound as all of them shouted their anthem in unison.

"Look at the mess that has been created," pointed out one of the waiters with a look of as much concern on his face as there is on a traffic policeman's face when the traffic signals stop working for some reason.

"Do not worry my friend, we are thirteen men but when we undertake any task, we work on it as one until we successfully finish it. We will clean it within ten minutes," replied Sooraj as the Brave Dogs quickly began to help the waiters with the clean up.

Shefali and her friends were quiet. She proceeded to pay the bill but the manager of Battlefield Café refused to accept any payment. He said, "Canada Singh has been sending his team for a team outing to our café every year a week before the prestigious tournament. Call it fan's love or a good gesture, but we never charge from his teams."

Ratandeep heard the manager and immediately informed Monty about it. "So that is why he sent us here. He knew that the Blasters would come here as a part of their rule. He wanted something to happen," said the captain. Ratandeep nodded.

Meanwhile Beta ran up to Shefali and apologized, despite the fact that she had taken his proposal as a non-hilarious joke. She apologized to him on the behalf of Zorawar for the slap. Hearing Shefali's melodious voice and watch her stand next to him was enough for Beta. He did not care about the words she used or the facial expressions she carried.

As Shefali, Tara and Tanmey proceeded towards the exit gate, Monty came up to them. He said, "Bruises are good as they leave temporary scars which can be diagnosed and treated easily. Heart breaks are not only internal but on most occasions long lasting. I can understand that your heart is bleeding and none can see it bleed. If by some chance, the Brave Dogs face the Southern Blasters on the ground, I do not know which team will you come out in support of but what I do know is that you will never disappoint anyone who loves you."

And then he requested them not to inform Canada about the unforeseen, dramatic incident and all three of them unanimously agreed. Anyway, Shefali was not going to tell her unsuspecting father either about the scuffle or about that slap by Zorawar. She was obviously not in any position to tell him about it. Wearing a mask of coping and normality, she left the café acting like nothing ever bothered the dad's princess.

10

BIRTHDAY GONE COMPLETELY WRONG

Friday, 12/June/2020

Two days to go to the start of the tournament

The heat wave of the sun during the day had forced Ganga barrage to outpour some of its water in the evening in order to maintain the river's water level. A matte black SUV strolled leisurely around the high and strong barrage. Courtesy the expensive woofers, the Punjabi music played in it as loud as the applause its singer would get after a scintillating performance on stage. After taking several rounds of the same road, the car finally crossed the famous 'I love Kanpur' attraction and headed towards the legendary Lovers' lane of Tilak Nagar passing through the Ganga Marg.

Though it was her birthday and she was dressed in her favorite black, solid knitted wrap dress presented to her almost a year ago by her loving father, Shefali, who accompanied Zorawar in the SUV, was noticeably not as happy and as optimistic as she would normally be. In fact, her characteristic smile was also missing from her pretty face and that concerned her boyfriend a lot.

"Is the weather hot or is it just you," said Zorawar trying hard to make her joyful but she did not react.

"I bought your favorite chocolate cake," he persevered.

"My father bought it too today morning."

"After winning it, I will dedicate The Pride of t20 cricket trophy to you."

"My father has picked Monty who is a good prospect for the trophy too."

"I love the V neck of your dress."

"My father loves it too," she replied looking out through the window.

"I like the stylish fabric belt around your waist."

"My father likes it too."

"But I know something that your father does not," he said and pulled the fabric belt to untie it and then gently pulled her towards him using his left hand round her fetchingly slim waist. Somehow this move cheered her up and she herself moved closer to him. It is only in moments like these that the automatic transmission cars score over the manual transmission ones.

With both audacious lovers feeling the magical warmth through the delicate touch and teddy bear like affectionate hugs, within five minutes they reached the Lovers' lane and parked the SUV between two other cars. The lane was around 300m long but just 5m wide.

The fact that there were just two street lights, one at entry and the other at exit, was enough to indicate how dark the lane was. Strictly following the unsaid but well understood rule, each car parked there had turned its headlamps off, perhaps for extra privacy, not just for themselves but for others as well.

Zorawar's thick, hedonistic lips brushed Shefali's. Neither was it sinless like a tease nor like the one by Bollywood stars in movies. It was hot, fiery, passionate, arousing and demanding, similar to the one by the shamelessly vigorous adult entertainers. She wanted to pull herself away before she lost herself but could not. All her practical senses had been irresistibly seduced and she could no longer think logically. "Baby, your lips are like red velvet pastry and it is time for me to eat them. Shefali, I love you a lot," he whispered slowly, purposely prolonging each word. She deliberately smiled with her heart fluttering at his masculine voice as she clasped her delicate and rosy palms on either side of his face. Never before had her name felt so wonderful. The couple leaned forward on one another.

Near the Lovers' lane was the Shakuni Children's Park where Monty and Canada had just finished an elaborate discussion on each and every detail of all the strategic plans which the Brave Dogs would follow going into the first match of the tournament. After the intense team brainstorming session, it was time for them to relax and in order to do so they decided to have a peg of whiskey together. They opted to enjoy it in Monty's Challenger so that Canada's wife does not try to break his head with a rolling pin on seeing him have a peg even on his self-declared non-drinking day.

"My wife Silky and I are looking for a good match for our serene and most beloved daughter Shefali," said Canada as Monty made a couple of big-hearted pegs, perhaps inspired by his recent visit to Patiala.

"She deserves a true and courteous knight on a white charger."

"It is tough to find them in the modern society. There is also a selfish fear in my head related to her marriage, and what if the chosen man is not good enough for her in the long run?"

"I think you must ask her about her choice."

"Though I think the champion cricketer Hemant is a suitable match for her, let us postpone this discussion till the end of the tournament. Buy a packet of potato chips to help us intake this peg. I prefer the classic salted one."

"Sure, I will show you the new grocery store too in the process."

"Take me from a short cut as I want chips as soon as possible."

"Sir, we will go through the Lovers' lane to reach there as fast as we can."

Without bothering to turn the left indicator on, Monty turned his Challenger into the Lovers' lane, completely unaware of the traumatic scene which was impatiently waiting for their clear and uninterrupted view.

Crossing a couple of parked but in motion cars, they indeed saw an unexpected and hopelessly tempestuous visual: a black SUV with a familiar couple unconditionally absorbed in one another, absolutely unaware about the surroundings. The girl in blue Punjabi suit had crawled over the handbrakes and was now facing her muscular man in front of the steering wheel. She had gripped his shoulders in her fists as they exchanged extremely hot, burning and glowing kiss. The way she slanted over him indicated that she did not want anyone to see her face, perhaps because it was blowing up inside, red and peppery.

"Slow down Monty, I have seen this lucky man somewhere," said Canada surprisingly trying his best to peep inside the parked car. Probably his neighbor Jamal aunty was his inspiration behind that gross act.

"Yes Sir, he is Jaganbir, our very own Brave Dog! He is busy with his girlfriend Sweety."

"Now I know why he wanted the practice session to get over quickly today! Naughty boy he is!" The smile from Canada was a sheepish one.

"Let it be Sir. Satisfied men perform better on the field than manual laborers anyway!"

"As a parent I am proud of my daughter. I know that never would she ever indulge in such practices unless I get her married to a knight with shining armor!"

And they drove a few meters ahead till they stopped parallel to Zorawar's black SUV. The scene inside that was somewhat similar to the one in Jaganbir's car, only the characters were different. It was indeed salaciously erotic, perhaps even indecent, obscene and titillating. Zorawar had used his sturdy hands to hold Shefali's round head, covering her ears with the press of his palms and simultaneously played gently with the strands of her untied hair. Maybe he hoped that the erased major lines of his palms would return soon if he continued playing with her like that.

It was not that Canada hated Zorawar. After all he had been the captain of Canada's own team for seven long years. Both obviously shared almost voluble affability between them. It was just that being the father of a daughter, he had an overpowering, overwhelming, devastating, fundamental need to keep her safe and pure. How can anyone expect a father to see his own offspring in a compromising situation and ignore it? Never can that be practical. He had seen Shefali as his princess, the one who loved teddy bears. Though Zorawar was a rich and well behaved guy apart from being a tremendous batsman, he was still a man, a real man, much different from a huggable soft toy.

There was a spontaneous crushing realization in Canada's mind that during the entire course of his life, he would not always be able to keep certain set of hormones out of his young daughter's body. But low level vulgarity was something that his eyes could not tolerate even for a second. Without thinking about the possible consequences, he opened the door of the Challenger, forcing Monty to suddenly apply breaks. He threw the glass carrying whiskey away, got down and banged his right hand straight against the door of the SUV, forcing the couple to separate from each other.

"I never came looking for a fistfight. I am a firm believer of non-violence, but no one stands back and quietly watches their child in such awkwardness, unless their own genes are defective. Mine are not," said Canada as he opened the door of the SUV and with all his physical strength, pulled Zorawar out, as if he was not a strong man but a lifeless toy.

Due to the sudden attack, the Southern Blasters' captain lost his balance and fell hips first on the road. Canada went on to ferociously slap his former student's stylishly bearded left cheek, so hard that some droplets of tear almost flowed out of his eyes. He then slapped him again, and again, and then again, all slaps striking the target harder than the previous one. The Punjabi words used by him actually hurt Zorawar more than those physical strikes by the middle aged coach. The slaps changed to short, horrible punches on the back and continued till Monty jumped out and managed to hold Canada. Never before in his professional career or even private life had the coach resorted to violence. Perhaps he did not know what a father should do when he unexpectedly catches his daughter with her boyfriend. It was a first for him too. Though Zorawar was a six pack abs gym freak, he was a really soft guy within. He could have easily pushed, punched or even kicked Canada but he did not. Perhaps it was due to the profound respect he had for the coach, or maybe due to the fact that he wanted that man to be his future father-in-law.

Shefali cried as if her brain was being mercilessly shredded from the inside. Emotional pain flowed out of every pore of her body. From her mouth came a cry, so raw that even the eyes of the completely stranger couples in other parked cars there were suddenly wet with tears. The sound of her cry was the one that humans are by default programmed not to ignore. Having lost all courage to show her face to her father, she buried it deep into a handkerchief and kept her eyes away from Canada. She grabbed onto the seat of the car so that her violent shaking would not cause her to fall.

Meanwhile, Zorawar stood up. The red eyes of the coach locked with his wet eyes as Canada said, "Speak up."

Without lowering his gaze by even a single degree, Zorawar replied, "Sir, you have been my cocoon for seven years and I thank you for every moment of it. Nowadays, when I practice batting or make crucial plans for my team, my eyes still wander in search of you. I gracefully accept the wrath of your slaps as the warmth of your hands imparted to me. Though they sting hard, they are indeed blessings in disguise. Your daughter rules over my heart and I love her unconditionally. She loves me too."

As Canada raised his right hand for another smack, Monty was quick to hold it again.

Zorawar continued, "Sir, I have the deepest and most reverential respect for you. I know you love Shefali a lot, but even you would agree that she has a life to live outside the circle of her house and parents."

"How long has this been going on?" Though Canada spoke clearly, his breaths were still deep and slow.

"Three years. I wanted to tell you but the Association instructed all the contracted players not to keep any kind of contact with you. Shefali and I had mutually decided not to disclose about our relationship to you till the end of the tournament. We did not want our love to be a hindrance in your unmatched efforts of setting up a new team from scratch and competing in ICC 2020 with your reputation not just at stake but in the hands of random unknown guys."

"Is this relationship physical?"

"Only kiss."

"I don't think you are the right guy for her."

"I don't think that there is anybody better than me for her."

"I have planned to get her married to Hemant, the Officers XI all rounder who I believe will win The Pride of t20 cricket trophy."

"Can a cricket trophy decide who will love Shefali more in the future?"

"I have a cement cricket bat and a ball built on the roof of my house. All my life, I have either played cricket or coached other players. My life begins and ends at cricket. The only thing I dream of is to win Incredible Cricket Championship. How can you expect me to marry my daughter to someone who has never won any significant trophy? Forget about you, even your team has never won anything. As far as I am concerned, I will marry Shefali to only a cricket champion."

"If that is how it would be, let me clear my side too. I feel it right into my bones that have got more than it takes to win it. My team Southern Blasters will emerge victorious and proudly lift the Incredible Cricket Championship 2020 trophy. I guarantee you that I will win The Pride of t20 cricket trophy. You know that I will put in all possible efforts to achieve what I have said. After that, I will marry my girlfriend Shefali and you should not have any problem with that."

"Yes my boy. If you win The Pride of t20 cricket trophy and your team wins the ICC 2020 then you get to marry Shefali too. You lose either of the trophies, you lose Shefali too. Best wishes to you and your team."

"The name is Bagga, Zorawar Bagga. After my team SB wins the tournament, we all will welcome SB into our group. The second SB stands for Shefali Bagga."

"Shefali cannot be compared to a trophy," interfered Monty, "she is a strong woman. Let her herself make the choice regarding her future."

Canada was in no mood to listen. He turned around and pushed Monty over the elongated bonnet of his Challenger to shut him up.

"But remember Zorawar," said Monty as he got up, "there is a new team in the mix this time. The Brave Dogs are coming to blow all of you away."

"See you on the ground!" said Zorawar. Surprisingly that remark from Monty brought a sarcastic smile on his face though it was overshadowed by the redness due to the slaps.

Shefali sat on the rear seat of the Challenger, next to the Pink Teddy Bear. Though her sobbing had considerably reduced, she was not in the frame of mind to understand or say anything. Usually over-expressive, at that time she had no courage to put up any expression on her shrunken face. This was perhaps the worst birthday she had ever celebrated. Could there be anything worse? She had no courage to participate in any type of conversation. She just could not gather it. Even her eardrums had stopped functioning. There was only the sickening, numbing, devastating, unspeakable and psychic pain to break her, enough to change her beyond recognition. She did not know if it was self inflicted one or no. She did not know what the future would be. She did not know if she would ever see Zorawar again. She did not know how she would face her father ever again in life. She did not know what her own reaction would be to the action taken by her mother when she reached home.

"Do whatever you want to do but do not trouble your mother and your father by slipping into depression," said Canada as Monty drove the Challenger out of the Lovers' lane leaving Zorawar alone with his SUV. That sentence from Canada was the only conversation they had till the time they reached home. Though Monty wanted to wish Shefali on the occasion of her birthday, he did not. He knew she would not even thank him if he did so.

11

Superstition (Kick Baba)

Saturday, 13/June/2020

One day to go to the start of the tournament

The foul smell of fresh human excrement entered into Dipshit's overly sensitive nose even before the sound of any crowing rooster could travel to his ears. He knew that leaving a neat towering pile of mud and a bucket half full of water on the footpath next to his own bedroom's window would serve as an open invitation to either a stray dog or a helpless man in emergency early in the morning. It was quite evident that repugnant smell was the alarm he often used when he did not want to disturb his sleeping parents. "Mustard oil pickled cauliflower," was the first thought in his mind as he woke up due to the disagreeable odour. He immediately turned the alarm off by closing the glassed window and walked towards his bathroom to get ready.

It was only ten minutes past six in the morning when he quietly walked out of his house. Taking giant sized steps, he proceeded towards the address provided by Kamlesh. On his way, he could see the sun cling to the roofs of the manmade structures and some of its light traipsing through the pyramids of toxic, mass-produced garbage that lay without any cover on either side of the road. "I am hopeful, hopeful for today, hopeful for tomorrow!" was the song he kept repeating inside his bell shaped head.

As he reached the construction site mentioned by Kamlesh, he looked for the famous YCB Backhoe Loader. Those machines are designed to be eye-catching and Dipshit could indeed see his destination within a minute behind that outrageous digger. It was merely a one room sized made-shift tent like arrangement with semi-constructed wings of the residential complex on all four sides. Perhaps that was the space left for the garden but that was its future. Presently, Kick Baba was using it to bless his covetous devotees.

"One, two, three... seventeen," Dipshit counted the number of devotees who had already taken their position before him. All those men were dressed in a pink lungi but were completely bare at the top. They had placed their usual clothes and belongings at a considerable distance, near the YCB digger. They were all sitting in a squatting position, similar to the one they sit when in an Indian style loo, with their backs turned towards Baba's tent. The smile on each of their transcendental faces proved that they believed smiling at obstacles was good as obstacles are nothing but bridges to success. Maybe each one of them had taken the social media good morning quotes a bit too seriously.

"Six hundred for the pink lungi, one thousand for the white one," said the square built, black bearded man sitting on a plastic chair next to the tent. He was probably Kick Baba's only assistant.

"That is much above the normal range. Can we bargain?" replied Dipshit observing the peculiar man from top to bottom.

"Then go back to your home. Baba kicks the person wearing a lungi only and white is his favorite color."

"Here is the consultation fee... I mean the money," Dipshit paid for it and on the instructions of the assistant, removed all his clothes, including the undergarments and wore just the new off-white lungi. He then joined the other smiling men. Facing opposite to the tent, he too sat in that squatting position with little attention towards his wallet and clothes.

"It is good that I eliminated all the waste material from my digestive tract via the anus, before coming here," he thought. Several minutes passed and then he heard the noise indicating some kind of movement behind his back.

Covering his entire brown skin with white talcum powder, Kick Baba was literally as thin as the layer of wafer biscuit on either side of the cream, but as tall as a common ostrich. Perhaps he was one of the biggest fans of a famous Tollywood actor and the way he wore the rectangular framed sunglasses after throwing it in the air was a proof of it. Though he was topless like his devotees, he too was wearing a lungi but a black colored one. His fairly large garland comprised of a dozen computer mouse sized fake human skulls made of clay. Usual skulls are bald but Kick Baba had stuck black painted cotton over each of them, possibly due to his eccentric fetish for hairy heads. His beard was completely black and reached till the middle of his oily chest. The hat he wore on his semicircular shaven head was red in color and had a large sized hairless clay human skull with a gigantic open mouth at its top and that probably served as a crown for the fully enlightened man.

The assistant was quick to play the famous 'Come into my home because I am stoned' song on the large sized Bluetooth speaker with the bass and volume already set to their maximum levels. The loud music was like liquid adrenaline being injected into Baba's blood stream. Probably he had never been to any dance class but it was obvious that he was used to dancing freely on that particular song. His moves had no deliberate intention to show off, to attract the enthusiastic devotees but nonetheless each one of them including Dipshit was impressed. Anyone, whose limbs were half as flexible as those of the non-materialistic Baba, would be a proud dancer himself.

When the song was about to reach its end, Kick Baba slowly danced his way behind the back of all his devotees and that was when the entertainment turned much serious for all the young men in lungi. Dipshit was indeed the lucky one as he received a gentle but well placed kick on his hips that made him fall face first into the soft gooey mud. The other men were visibly disappointed as they had to wait longer for their turn as the assistant signaled Dipshit to go into the tent and discuss his problems with the Baba.

The sun was already shining outside but inside the tent, it was as dark as it was still midnight. The only source of light was a candle that was lit in the middle of a tiny round table and but it was not enough to see anything apart from each other's face. There were no chairs and Dipshit once again sat in a squatting position opposite to the Baba, trying to wipe the mud off his face with the lower portion of the lungi.

"My dear young man, what attracts you to me?" Baba's accent, facial expressions and body language was similar to a famous nepotism enthusiast Bollywood director and that really shook Dipshit deep within as he did not expect such a coincidence, if that could be termed as one. "Most people can draw straight lines, but some can't because they are..." was mentioned on a poster kept next to the candle on the table. Surprisingly, the last word was missing from the six inch long poster. Dipshit was quick to read it while Baba was engrossed in thinking something.

"Baba I have been selected as a batsman in a cricket team and will be playing professional cricket for the first time in my life. Please help me play well and make a name for myself," he replied but his words were not clear as he was a bit frightened by the uncanny darkness and ominous silence inside the tent.

"Come closer to me and whisper the name of your coach in my ear," said Baba looking voraciously at the left over mud on his devotee's nose.

Though Dipshit initially hesitated, considering the fact that he had purchased an overpriced off-white lungi for that particular interaction, he did not have any other option. "Cunth Dhaar Singh," he unconvincingly whispered trying his best to maintain at least one arm's distance from the Baba, who felt the tickle but did not tilt his head by more than half a degree.

"I am sorry but your team will not win the tournament," the Baba was clear and concise with his prediction. He then pushed Dipshit away and widened his own eyes. Inhaling a deep breath, he swiftly moved both his hands behind his back and pointed his chest forward. He then pulled out a couple of plastic flowers, one pink and the other white, that were probably hidden somewhere behind him.

"I have two, choose one."

Remembering the words of the assistant regarding the Baba's favorite color and also the suggestion by Kamlesh, Dipshit chose the white one but the Baba was clearly not happy with his choice. He threw the chosen white one backwards and horizontally placed the pink one in the open mouth of the hairless skull on his hat.

"Don't you have a boyfriend?" he said as his tongue rolled out momentarily from his mouth and there was a bit of acceleration in his breathing rate.

"I am heterosexual and don't need any medical certificates to prove that," replied Dipshit, who had already developed a sensation of pins and needles in his feet. His voice was an indication of his dry throat.

"So, do you have a girlfriend?"

"There is a girl but I have not proposed her yet."

"Thank God!" exclaimed Baba as he opened his eyes possibly as wide as any human can open them. After letting out a long, exasperated sigh, he continued, "The stars are not in your favor at the moment. Maintain a smile at your girl's face at all times during your match if you want to shape your future in professional cricket. This will also help your team to emerge victorious. Always wear a white pearl ring while batting. That will protect you from getting out. And the most important thing, propose her only after the tournament ends so that you can concentrate on one thing at a time. Now take a couple of steps back and turn around."

"Thank you Baba," said Dipshit and then like an obedient front row scholastic student, he turned his back towards the Baba, maintaining the squat perfectly despite the tingling in his feet. Once again, there was a gentle yet well placed kick on his hips that made him fall face first but the mud there was comparatively less gooey.

He dragged his body out without turning back and tried to wipe his face with the lungi but immediately realized that pulling it up would expose him more than he would have liked to. Quickly he changed back to his clothes. The wallet and the underwear were no longer there and when he complained to the assistant, the only reply he got was, "Read that board." There was a tiny placard that lay face down near the YCB digger. It read, "You are yourself responsible for all your belongings."

Dipshit looked towards the closed zip of his trouser and realized that though his wallet containing two hundred rupees and an underwear with a small hole at the back were missing, he had at least not been robbed of something more precious. Without any argument, he ran away from that predatory place towards his house.

12
Match 1:
Brave Dogs v Gorillas

Sunday, 14/June/2020

The surprisingly impressive and deafening noise made by the thrilled crowd at the start of the Incredible Cricket Championship, 2020 would never be suggestive of their numbers. There were around one thousand five hundred people but they were as loud as fifteen thousand. Judging by the brown jerseys all over, it was quite evident that the majority of them were cheering for the Gorillas. There could be a billion audience members but what Canada cared for at that moment was just controlled aggression and fair play from his boys.

"We will bowl first," said Monty as he won the coin toss. The pitch had no tinge of grass and as expected, it looked like a batting friendly one. Clearly, the conditions had no role to play in their decision. It was just that batting with a target in sight somewhat reduces the pressure, especially in first ever professional cricket match appearance of a team with eleven debutants.

With a famous Punjabi song almost blowing away each of the speakers in the stadium, the Brave Dogs made a grand entry into the field of play, led by their captain. As they grouped into a team huddle, Monty said, "We will follow Plan A as long as we can. The coach and I will decide if and when to switch to Plan B." Although all of them shook their heads, Beta was the only one who did not seem impressed. "Woof, woof, woof!" All of them shouted simultaneously, accompanied by the bench strength duo and the coach from the dugout, and then each of them jogged towards his pre allotted fielding position.

Both the opening batsmen from the Gorillas were left handed. As discussed in the team meeting prior to the match, Monty threw the ball to his leg spinner Pappu and reminded him to mix them up.

Pappu could not catch it cleanly and the unruly crowd started with some provocative jeering even before the first ball was bowled.

"Play," said the young umpire as loud as he could to start the first match of the tournament.

Not only were Pappu's palms sweaty, even his legs and arms began to feel weak as he stood motionless like a torpid figure cut in stone. Perhaps his mind was no longer in the state of a soft panic. It had grown up into heavy breathing. He clearly remembered each and every delivery he had practiced. He even wanted to bowl but his feet just froze at one place as if he had stepped on the wet cement floor and forgot to move till it dried. The jibes from the crowd got louder. The batsmen, fielders and the umpire were all telling him to bowl but he had choked up so much that he could not react or even say a word.

"We are without a doctor. Come on Pappu, bowl now," screamed the squatting Sooraj from the opposite side of the pitch.

"Change the bowler, send him here," shouted Canada from the dugout as the twelfth man Ratandeep ran into the field with the coach's message.

"Go Pappu, go to the dugout immediately. Beta Kumar vacate the slip. You will open the attack. Ratandeep be ready to grab the ball at the first slip," Monty said with both his arms raised, indicating to each of the team member that the Brave Dogs would begin the contest with Plan B instead of A. Pappu somehow managed to jog out of the ground amidst the jeers, not raising his eyes above the level of his new pair of shoes.

The first delivery from the team's number one swing bowler Beta was a wild one down the leg and even Sooraj could not collect it behind the stumps forcing the umpire to signal five wides, probably the worst way to start the proceedings. The entire first over was unexpectedly wayward and ended up yielding fifteen runs, a new record for the most expensive first over in Kanpur's local cricket history.

Every player including the captain Monty appeared as confused as the student who cannot decide between making notes and memorizing the theory a day before the examination. It was purely the rich experience of Canada Singh which prevented their shoulders from dropping. Though he did not step ahead the boundary rope, he sent Sarfaraz with the message that if they stick to their plan, the curious confusion would pass through just like the sea waves reside after a high tide and assured them that Pappu would be back on the field soon.

"What went wrong Pappu? You bowled so well in the practice sessions," Canada tried his best to maintain calm though internally he was a bit nervous.

"Oh Pappu," said Sarfaraz, "I too choked up when I visited a posh coffee shop with my friends for the first time. I was sort of frightened to order thinking that the waiter might make fun of me because of my background. I can understand your emotions right now but trust me this is just something randomly cooked up by your own mind. It is so tasteless that others won't even eat it."

"Shut up Sarfaraz," shouted Canada and then changed his tone into a normal one and said, "Pappu, do you know why A is like a flower?" Sarfaraz's reaction was similar to the one he would have on his face if someone just fired a bullet next to him. And then Canada burst into an unrestrained laughter, unable to control himself. Even the panic stricken lad looked at his coach. "Sir, at least finish the joke," said Sarfaraz finding his voice after a minute.

"It is because B follows it!"

The eyes of Pappu and Sarfaraz locked over with a soft expression of faint and humorless smile. "Yeah, this is what I wanted," said Canada, "Pappu, now you must name any three people from our team and then any three sounds you hear."

"Beta, Sarfaraz and Alpha... I hear the noise generated by the crowd, your voice and the pleasant sound made by the bat and ball on their collision," Pappu said as he turned his head towards the field where the batsman just hit a splendid four on Jaganbir's third delivery.

"Good, now shake your legs, ankles and arms."

"I want to play, I want to bowl. I just got frightened with thousands of eyes from all sides looking at me," said Pappu, kicking the air with his legs and punching it too with his clenched fists, in a considerable frustration that had built up in his mind but had no opening to release itself.

"The 3-3-3 rule always works," said Canada to Sarfaraz and then he turned towards Pappu, "Go, play and keep talking to yourself on the field. The more you speak and think positive, the easier it would be to keep anxiety out of your head. Remember, talk only about topics which do not make you feel nervous. You are our trump card. Go, break this partnership and bring us back in the game."

As the fourth over ended, Pappu was back on the field and that lifted the morale of the other Brave Dogs to some extent. Beta and Jaganbir had taken a lot of stick in their two overs and Monty did not delay a bit to introduce leg spin against the hard hitting pair of batsmen. This time, hope sat on Pappu's skin just like winter dew on the green grass. Perhaps the famous Bollywood song he repeated in a rhythmic phrase gave him the confidence to perform to the best of his abilities. Though he could not pick a wicket in his first over, he did manage to control the flow of runs to some extent giving away only four singles in the over.

The first half of the innings completed with 112 runs on the board and without any wicket down. The crowd had realized that this was going to be a complete one sided match. The illegal betting mafia would have also given up on this one as the result was so obvious.

"The coach has instructed to move Dipshit to long on," said Ratandeep who was once again on the field with a bottle of water for the friend cum captain, Monty.

"But he is fielding well at third man. Why to make him jog across the entire diameter of the ground?"

"Canada Sir has said."

And then Monty swapped the fielding positions of Dipshit and Junaid, both of whom were clearly not impressed by the strange decision.

Running out of options, the captain finally turned to his unpredictable man. Though he was not anywhere close to being a decent bowler, he was somehow the coach's favorite.

What a start it was for Kalee. His first delivery in any form of cricket match and he struck! The joy on the faces of the bowler, fielders and even the coach in the dugout was simply incredible. The ball pitched on the leg stump but straightened a little forcing the batsman to miss the flick. It would have definitely gone on to hit the middle of the middle stump. Perhaps that was the breakthrough needed so desperately by the Brave Dogs. The very next ball was a masterpiece too. A quick and well directed bouncer forced a pull shot by the new batsman, who was never in control of it. A faint edge and Sooraj dived to his left catching the ball with minimum effort as if wicketkeeping was something he did every day. The hat trick ball was a slower one which went straight on and even the experienced left hander could not read it. The ball successfully pierced through the wide gap between bat and pad to kiss the off stump. A hat trick on the first three balls was something that none of the contracted players competing in the tournament had managed to achieve at the start of their careers.

Perhaps Kalee did not know how to celebrate. He simply stood at one place staring at the coach, who was up on his feet in the dugout to applaud the accomplishment. The mid off fielder Kunal was the first person to hug his bowler. It was not a hug of gentle arms that leaves ample space to breathe. It was a hug of strong arms that tells the body, brain and soul that the person is actually happy for your achievement.

The good vibrations from the Brave Dogs were an outburst of the calm after the inner storm that they had just encountered. For the first time in match, they got together near the pitch and each one of them shouted their anthem, "Woof, woof, woof," with an air of confidence in their voice. The members of the crowd had lost their voice a couple of deliveries ago, but some of them stood up and clapped for the Brave Dogs. That reaction almost made a drop of tear fall from the eyes of Canada Singh but somehow he controlled his emotions and opted just to clap softly for his players including the bench strength.

On the instructions of the coach, Monty changed the field from defensive to an attacking one by bringing more fielders close in to apply pressure on the new batsmen. The motive was not to allow easy singles and doubles. The spinners Pappu and Alpha were successful in restricting the flow of runs while Kalee's variations turned out to be too tough to decode for the Gorillas as he ended up picking a five wicket haul in his quota of four overs.

It was indeed an innings of two halves which were not at all similar to each other. If one was North Pole, the other was South Pole. The Gorillas ended with just 156/8, with Beta Kumar chipping in for a couple of tidy overs and two wickets at the death, thereby earning the chance to look into the eyes of his captain as they walked out of the playing area like a pack of wolves returning after a successful hunt. Half of the crowd was now on their side after their exceptional recovery and the illegal betting mafia had already taken out their books again. The good contest between bat and ball overshadowed the absence of the cheerleaders and that was a positive as far as the tournament organizers and sponsors were concerned.

"Well played boys," Canada welcomed his players with a pat on the back of the shoulder of each one of them.

"I personally have the experience of watching the Gorillas' fast bowlers. They are really quick but struggle to pitch the ball in the right areas. Dipshit and Kunal, you guys have to go hard at them at the start of the innings. We can break this into four parts of five overs each. Our first aim would be to score around forty runs in the first five without losing a wicket. They would introduce spin if their pacers are unable to strike. Their main left arm spinner Pandey can really turn the ball both ways. Beware of going out of the crease against him. I believe we have already done the difficult part of containing them to a below par total. Now, all we need to do is to be smart." The coach delivered his last minute guidelines, trying to speak as much as he could in the five minute break. Some players compared the speed of his words to the running speed of the cartoon which moves out of focus leaving behind a fuzzy trail along its path.

"Come on boys, let us do it!" exclaimed Monty as Dipshit and Kunal padded up, ready to face the attack by the Gorillas.

The sound of the firecrackers was a signal to the batsmen to sprint towards the pitch and the rest of the team to take their positions in the dugout. It was a moment of embarrassment for Kunal as he almost reached the batting crease but Dipshit did not put a step beyond the boundary rope.

"It seems your mate is already afraid of facing our lethal bowling," said one of the Gorillas' fielders to Kunal, who just responded with a blow of hot air out his mouth. Perhaps the only thing the Brave Dogs did not learn during those long training sessions was how to cope up with the on field sledging.

"What is the matter with you?" The furious coach said as he almost pushed his batsman towards the playing area.

"I am not anxious for sure," replied Dipshit, "I am not hyper or restless. I can even concentrate well but in order to be comfortable wearing these batting gloves, I have taken off my lucky charm - the white pearl ring from my right digitus medius. It was fine for the practice sessions, but I think I need it for the match."

"Digitus medius?" said a couple of players looking for an answer from each other but did not get it until they saw an infuriated Kunal pointing his digitus medius from the pitch towards Dipshit.

"Where is it? Wear it. This is not the time you can afford to waste," said Monty.

"Ever heard of a time-out rule?" questioned Kamlesh with a look of urgency on his face as he scratched his head near the *choti*.

"I do not think this is a case of short term memory loss but I forgot where I kept it. I think we all must try to find it as soon as we can," said Dipshit. He sounded as concerned as a little kid getting his first haircut.

Canada had had enough. He had seen a lot of superstitious players throughout his long and bustling career but never had he seen someone delaying the start of the innings for an object that had no logical connection at all with the sport. At the same time, he knew that getting completely into the face of his opening batsman would create a sort of panic into the latter's head. The coach did not want to add to the pressure the batsman was already under. To calm Dipshit down, he said, "Go and bat out there with utmost and undisturbed concentration. We will search for your ring and send it to you as soon as we find it."

Dipshit was sure that the coach had more in his mind than he let on, but unlike some of the others, he would never say that in an attempt to belittle the intensity of his mentor's feelings. And he decided to walk into the playing area with a bare digitus medius. This was one of Canada's bigger moments to cherish as he could see respect for himself in his player's eyes as he went out to bat, full of unconquerable confidence even without his white pearl ring. Meanwhile, he instructed Jaganbir and Junaid to search for the ring in Dipshit's kitbag.

"I am surprised how a guy of such a low IQ can be a medical student?" said Premi, the hard hitting left hand opening batsman and the wicketkeeper of the Gorillas, as Dipshit got ready to face the first delivery of the innings. When a person sees, feels or hears something that frightens him, a primitive part of the brain is activated to produce aggression. The first ball was a slower bouncer gone wrong. Dipshit picked it early to smoke it over deep midwicket for a six with a powerful pull shot. Perhaps that shot was his reply to the foul mouthed wicketkeeper. He turned with his back facing towards Premi and pointed at his own name on his jersey, leaving the glove man red faced.

The banter got the crowd going and that pleased the coach and the captain a lot. However, the Brave Dogs dugout was still a nervous place to be in. Some of them sat still as they thought moving an inch could result in the loss of a wicket. Canada Singh was up on his feet and decided to walk in a loop between the boundary rope and his seat. When he sat, his legs would shake and force him to continue his walk. Though he was the eldest one out there, the energy and enthusiasm he had would put many teens to shame.

Meanwhile Junaid found the lost ring and informed the others. Canada instructed that at the end of the first over, Ratandeep would run to the pitch and hand it over to Dipshit.

Kunal on the other hand, was finding it tough to rotate the strike or even hit a boundary. After playing three dot balls on a trot, he decided to chip a full delivery towards deep cover for a single creating an easy chance for the fielder, but the generous fielder presented him a much needed gift. He put down a sitter. The batsmen quickly scampered through for a run, taking Kunal off the mark with a nervous smile on his lips.

Dipshit got his ring back and quickly wore it under the glove. Kunal for some reason refused to take singles, although they were available on two successive deliveries of the second over. That made Canada as furious as a football coach when his player misses an easy goal. He took out his spiral diary to note down something in it, uttering a few cuss words aimed at Kunal, which obviously did not reach the batsman amidst the deafening noise made by the crowd. He then turned to the other teammates and yelled, "This is exactly what none of you should do when you are batting out there. Trust your partner at the other end. Look at that magician who thinks he should face all the balls. I know he owns a couple of bats but here is a cricket match to be won and this is a team sport. Dipshit is playing well and at the moment it is in the interest of the team to give him as much strike as possible."

Finally, Kunal took a single on the fourth ball of the over thinking there could be two but not to be. Dipshit was obviously under pressure to score big off the final two deliveries, but what soothed him was the fact that the ring was now under his glove and therefore, he took a couple of premeditative steps ahead the crease for the slog but missed it by daylight between the ball and the bat. The ball in fact angled in and went on to dismiss the bails by just a minor brush against the off stump.

"I will never wear this ring again," said Dipshit on his long walk back to the dugout as Monty made his way to the middle, surprisingly wearing a cap instead of helmet. He started his batting campaign in the ICC 2020 by defending the first ball from the lanky fast bowler striking it with the sweet spot on the middle of his bat. The collision of ball and bat made one of the most pleasant sounds one could ever hear on a cricket field.

"Irrational thought is the main cause of superstition. You played well when you were not thinking about the ring. The moment it was in your finger, you decided to take some risks thinking it would save you. The change in your mind led to a change in your approach and that resulted in the fall of your wicket," Canada explained Dipshit keeping as cool as the 2011 cricket world cup winning Indian captain even during the tricky situation of the match.

The batting display by Monty and Kunal was of poor quality. It was as if the two were out there to survive a complete session of test match cricket despite some ordinary bowling from the Gorillas. Though they found the middle of the bat on many occasions, they just could not place it in the gaps. Even the bowlers seem to enjoy it as the required run rate increased to a massive twelve runs per over for the last ten overs. That was when pressure got to Kunal and in an attempt to drive past the cover region he edged a wide delivery straight into the hands of the first slip. Along with the public, the illegal bookies too seemed to be bored as the match had once again completely switched to being a one-sided affair.

Kamlesh, Junaid, Alpha and even Sooraj to some extent tried their best to slog and even managed to send a few flying into the crowd and that earned some respect for the Brave Dogs. At least they were going down fighting. On the instructions of the coach, all they strived to do was to hit massive sixes out of the park on every ball they faced. They came to bat one after the other, slogged a few and then perished. Monty on the other hand kept his test match mode activated but continued to take regular ones and twos. Somehow, the Gorillas could not manage to take his wicket till the last over of the match.

As Sooraj missed a rather straight ball that went on to uproot the middle stump, the scorecard read 140/6 at the end of 19 overs. There had been an intense argument in the dugout as to why Sooraj was promoted ahead of Beta during such a make or break situation of the match but obviously the coach had the final say. That move perhaps could have proved disaster for the Brave Dogs if Sooraj was not dismissed as their eldest player really struggled to clear the fence apart from an odd four of bottom of the bat towards the vacant third man region.

To calm the nerves after the argument, Canada said to his last recognized batsman Beta, "There was once a horse that was held captive from the time it was just two months old. After several years of slavery, one fine day the rusty chains were replaced by an ordinary silk thread. It did not escape, thinking that it was born to be tied that way. Beta, my boy, you have two options. A- You think we have already lost this match and just bat out the remaining balls and B - You think we are going to win and you just need to complete the formalities."

"I opt for option C- Break the shackles and turn them to your weapon!" said Beta as he picked up the bat and walked out to the middle without even wearing a helmet. Perhaps that way he could read the fielding positions better. Canada had worked extremely hard to instill that kind of confidence into his boys and the optimistic attitude of Beta assured him that his coaching still had its fire power intact.

Pandey was indeed the bowler chosen by the Gorillas for the final over, as predicted by Canada Singh in the dugout, three overs ago.

"Go for it on the leg side," said Monty to his new partner.

"I am not going to follow any advice from a selfish player batting on forty of as many balls in a t20 match and on top of that has not hit a boundary yet," said Beta with a stare directed straight into the two black gemstones.

"Do it the way you want but make sure that it is done," replied the captain, surprisingly with a smile instead of tension on his bearded face.

The electric bullets were dodged to perfection by Monty till that moment but he could not successfully read the slow velocity pellet from Pandey. He wanted to cut it for his first boundary but got a thick outer edge. The ball flew off, only to land safely into the experienced hands of short third. That was exactly what Canada and the rest of the Brave Dogs did not want at that stage. Luckily, the batsman crossed while the ball was in the air and that meant Beta would be on strike for the next delivery as Jaganbir wore his Mohawk spiked helmet to join the right hander.

"Scarlett is still alive," commented one of the fielders as Monty walked towards the dugout with his head hung down and lips making a pout. It was obviously an outburst of disappointment, not a pose for any of the social media selfies.

"Well played Monty but bad luck," the coach welcomed his captain to the dugout. The positive remark came as a surprise for many team members. "How much does Sir back him," were some of the murmurs but not for long as there was an incredible competition going on.

The next three balls from Pandey were identical - fuller in length and tossed high up in trajectory. The result of each of them was also identical - a powerful slog sweep over the deep square leg fielder's head for a monumental six.

There was an absolute paralysis for a couple of seconds due to happiness, joy and pride, all at the same time in the Brave Dogs camp and exactly the opposite in their much experienced counterparts' dugout. Nobody on the field could conceal their emotions. Out of nowhere, Canada's boys had made it to the next stage of the tournament. The adrenaline rush was converted to an excess secretion of endorphins inside the body of each Brave Dog. Beta and Jaganbir came running to join the team huddle that was formed not for saying or listening to anything, but for getting together for their anthem. Each one of them raised his voice to its maximum level, "Woof, woof, woof."

Though the boys were jumping, singing, hugging and swinging arms, Canada Singh felt something new. Numerous invisible thorns had been poked in his skin for over a year and suddenly all his tension leeched out. His steps felt lighter as he tilted his face towards the members of the crowd, who were on their feet applauding the heroic effort by the lowest ranked team of the tournament.

"That was a master stroke from you Sir," said Kamlesh referring to the strategic move of holding back Beta for the death overs, not just with the ball but also with the bat.

"There was nothing extra ordinary in that Kamlesh. I demoted him down the order because he has grown up playing left arm spin of his brother Alpha. I knew that Gorillas would bowl Pandey at the end and his left arm spin would not trouble Beta as much as it would to our other players," it was not Canada but his experience that answered Kamlesh.

With a triumphant smile that appeared broader than the size of his entire face, Beta collected the man of the match trophy from a renowned IAS officer. On the request by the ground's men, the players walked into the dressing room to celebrate their achievement.

13

THE TRAITOR

Sunday, 14/June/2020

"**D**o not celebrate so much. Conserve your energies for the next game. It is extremely regrettable but I have no other option but to disclose this to all of you. There is a player in our team who is excessively clever and obviously he is right now within the walls of this dressing room. He is the one who audaciously disclosed our secret game plans to the opponents," said Canada as he sat on a green foldable steel chair after storming into the dressing room.

None of the Brave Dogs had expected to hear such words, especially after winning the first match by the barest of all margins. It had been a while since the squad had seen that kind of rage from their coach. The wrath expelled slower than magma but the smooth, inelegant blend of some Punjabi derogatory words in his speech made it just as destructive. Though involuntary, both his hands displayed a strange kind of a quivering movement.

All the eyes along with raised brows turned towards Sarfaraz and Junaid, probably because both the unblinking individuals were sporting an over innocent look, similar to that of wondrously productive cows at a dairy. The abrupt change in Sarfaraz's reaction ostentatiously displayed the magnitude of fear that had slipped into his transparent mind. He took a sudden intake of breath and stumbled backwards, jamming his heel into the wooden bench behind him. His frightened shoulders shook as he held hands firmly with his best friend Junaid.

"You work at The Powerful Horse Boutique as an assistant of Master Shams-ud-din, don't you?" said the champion Beta Kumar surprisingly without any sign of commendable modesty. His eyes though had a look of internal vexation that made it evident that he had swallowed anger when it was fire-seed and forgot to drink something cool. It grew in his belly and came out as hot as any fearsome dragon would ever flame.

"I told you Sir, not to trust these two. Sarfaraz is your enemy Master Shams-ud-din's faithful aide and though he is in our team, he is here to play against us. May God give us the strength to get over this insensitive betrayal," Ratandeep too seemed to support Beta.

"Say that you did not leak our plans otherwise we all will take turns to slap you. I will personally smack eight backhand slaps but count as one," Sooraj teamed up, throwing his abdominal guard on the floor in order to free his hands for maximum impact.

"Shut up all of you. First make sure whether these two are the real culprits or no," said Kunal, sounding the most mature one amongst the heated minds in that dressing room.

Trying his best to keep effectual check over his own bestial anger, Canada said, "It is better not to name anybody without substantial proof. Unfortunately, it is unquestionable that there is a traitor right now in this dressing room. We are a team of gifted amateurs playing in this tournament as professionals. Though we are fourteen unique individuals, we need to be one unit. I am not talking about entire life. I am talking only about this tournament. Are we so weak that we have trust issues among ourselves? We have an investigator and a psychological illusionist in our team too. It will hardly take five minutes to catch the culprit. Do you think we must go through that route?"

"Who said the illusionist cannot be a traitor," said Alpha, staring straight into Kunal's eyes, as if he had solved the disturbing conundrum in one sentence.

Beta Kumar had been silent for long. Adding insult to injury, he said, "Our captain, the great investigator, Monty is a womanizer and a former drug addict. The way he batted can be an indication that he is the one. The women supporting the Gorillas were anyway beautiful."

"Shut up all of you," screamed Canada with both his palms touching his forehead in an expression of profound disgust. He picked up a bottle of water and drank the entire litre of the liquid in just a couple of sips. Certainly, it was not to quench his agonizing thirst but perhaps to mask his frantic frustration over the political divide that still existed within his team and the emergence of an insolent traitor out of nowhere during the match.

"As our highly admired coach said, we are a team of gifted amateurs. He has given us an unexpected but marvelous opportunity to play as professionals and compete against some of the strongest cricket teams of the town during the course of this coveted tournament. We should definitely be thankful to him. This is also our moment to get together and play not just for victory but also for pride. We managed to win today and that many would say was a quirky one-time fluke but I don't think so. Thanks to Canada Sir's invaluable and ingenious tips and also the rigorous training schedule, we were able to beat the Gorillas. We won because we were successful in creating pressure on them and they faltered. Let us not publically name the wrongdoer. I have observed the body language of each one of us and I think I already know who the culprit is. I request him to meet Canada Sir and me in person after we disperse today." Monty sounded impeccably logical as he always did, though Beta Kumar was not much pleased with his captain's words. He was possibly of the opinion that he would get the sole credit for their unpredicted win.

"Before we disperse, with complete faith in fate, I would like to thank the Almighty who chose us as members of this wonderful team. We have prayed for our victory here in this dressing room. Going against own team is a sin. Is it even possible that we think our prayers will be answered by the Almighty if we are so wicked and immoral in practical life?" said Junaid as the pillow of fear that seemed to cover his mouth and nose for quite some time now appeared to fade away quickly.

"I agree with Junaid and assure all of you that even though my boss, Master Shams-ud-din is an old and formidable enemy of our respected coach, neither the Master nor I will ever be involved in any act that questions fair play." Sarfaraz too seemed to have found his voice back.

"That's the spirit," said Kunal, who had been observing everyone closely thus far.

"Squad, disperse. Tomorrow is a rest day for all of us. We will gather the day after at 11AM for a practice session before the next match. The betrayer is free to meet Monty and me in person before that. We promise this would not be discussed ever again," said Canada in his usual crisp and rhythmic accent.

"You may think we are the underdogs but no, no, no! We are the Brave Dogs, the mighty mighty Brave Dogs! Woof, woof, woof!" The echo generated by the enthusiastic voice of thirteen young men and a middle aged man inside the dressing room was expectedly not a harmonious one but quite surreal.

The squad dispersed in groups of two and three taking their water bottles with them, leaving behind the coach and the captain in peace to discuss the grave issue between them.

"Now I know why you instructed me to move Dipshit to the opposite side of the field," said Monty to Canada, who still had a concerned look over his face.

"I am experienced enough Monty. I have seen such cases before. But, never ever even in my dreams did I expect anything of this sort from a member of this particular squad. You know very well how hard I have worked to create this team. If there is a betrayal by my player at this stage of the tournament, I think it is my fault as a coach. I have erred somewhere and failed to instill the team spirit in my boys." And then the dressing room slipped into an awkward silence with both of them finding no words to say.

"I am sorry Monty and Canada Sir," said Dipshit, entering quietly into the dressing room with his head held down. An eerie, unbearable tension was evident on his face and limbs. It was quite possible that his mind played replays of something in a loop, something he desperately wanted to forget. His breathing became high speed and shallow as he approached towards the coach. Falling almost flat on Canada's feet, he repeated, "I am sorry. Please forgive me. It will never be repeated."

As he stood up, Canada wrapped his own hands around Dipshit's back and pulled him closer. He could feel the culprit's body shake like a leaf, tremble like a mobile phone set on vibration. Even his tiny eyes had almost swelled up with the droplets of tears and perhaps that is what restricted him from looking into the coach's eye.

"We are here to create a story and you tried to be the bloody villain in that. It is tough to digest that a person like you can be a traitor. You even know how much I hate being betrayed and still you could not stop yourself. However, it is good that you have realized your mistake, Dipshit," Monty tried to start the conversation, though he did not appear to be fully convinced by Dipshit's oddly courteous apology.

"Why?" asked the coach patting the back of his player, just like any middle class Indian father would do after an intense round of slaps on the unblemished cheeks of his son.

"I did it to make Pornika smile. My intention was not to betray my own team. I realized this grave mistake after the match ended, just had no courage to speak up in front of the entire squad. I was scared, too scared. What if we had lost the match due to my silliness?"

The coach looked like he was one of the pop eyed toy from the claw machine at the fun fair. Surprised and more so because Dipshit could not use any medical terminology to explain his foolishness, he simply asked, "Who is Pornika?"

"She is my girlfriend. She is the biological sister of Premi, the Gorillas' opening batsman and wicketkeeper. I only wanted to make her smile by letting her brother do well in the match. Trust me I did not want us to lose."

Monty and Canada exchanged a long eye contact and then Monty said, "Are you truly in love with her?"

"Yes, I will propose her soon."

"Does she love you?"

"I am sure she will say yes to my proposal."

"Dipshit," interrupted the captain, "had she been in true love with you, she would have liked to see you play well. The result would not have mattered to her."

"She did not order me to help Premi. It was just a stupid, really laughable thought in my mind that she would smile if her brother plays well. She looks more beautiful with a charming smile on her face. I love her dimples."

"You are a mad man."

"Yes, even I think so now. Blindly following a suggestion from Kamlesh, I went to Kick Baba who instructed me to do everything possible to maintain a smile on her gorgeous face. But Sirs, I assure both of you that I have just one crush at the moment and the Gorillas have been knocked out of the tournament already."

The strict disciplinarian in Canada had died few moments ago and in his place was a happy coach after his team's victory. And so, he did what happy coaches do. "The strangest part is that a medical student like you fell in the trap laid by an illiterate, fraud *baba*. See you on the practice day. Invite Pornika for our next match, we need some glamorous cheers from the crowd!"

"I have thrown the white pearl ring into the dustbin and with it all the advice given to me by Kick Baba! She will surely be there for all our matches and I would propose her with a ring hidden in the trophy after we win the final! Woof, woof, woof!"

"That's more like my Brave Dog," said the coach in a jovial mood. If there ever was a man who loved and held compassion and kindness as his highest treasures, it was Canada Singh.

The three content souls left the stadium in Monty's outlandish Challenger with Dipshit occupying the rear seat next to the Pink Teddy Bear.

14

MATCH 2:
BRAVE DOGS V
OFFICERS XI

Saturday, 20/June/2020

Among the sea of green in the jovial crowd, there was a small group of exuberant spectators cheering for the men in red. Canada Singh, Dipshit, Jaganbir, Beta and Kalee believed that the sudden, newfound respect and willing support of the people were earned by them through their competent performance in the first match. However other Brave Dogs including Monty were still skeptical because of the fact that Pornika and Sweety were the ones leading the red jersey support campaign.

The long legged damsel, Pornika was dressed in a slinky maroon off shoulder side split dress with long sleeves while the blue eyed bombshell, Sweety was in bridal lehenga like red Punjabi suit complimenting the colorful set of plastic bangles on her forearms. Though Tanmey and Tara were amongst the spectators too for the weekend match, they were hardly visible from the dugout.

The Brave Dogs finished giving birthday style bumps to Dipshit and Jaganbir and then Canada started with his last minute success mantras and ingenious tips. Meanwhile amidst the customary full throated cheer from all sections of the crowd, the two enigmatic captains walked out briskly for the coin toss.

Had there been anybody other than Monty, the businesslike confidence and belligerent attitude of the defending champions Officers XI's skipper Hemant would have definitely put his opponent on back foot even before the first ball was bowled. No wonder he was nicknamed 'The Ant' by his friends. The sheer strength he seemed to possess was similar to those of the ants who easily carry food, multiple times heavier than their own bodies. Despite the widespread gossip that he was a pure vegan, his muscles were suggestive of the hours he spent daily training hard at the gym. There was an animated spark in him with kinetic energy oozing out of his body like effervescence from a shaken bottle of soda. Perhaps that was the prime quality which forced Canada to think about marrying Shefali to him.

Hemant called it correct and opted to bat first. The Brave Dogs took the field with the recently established belief that they could do it again. Concurrently, in the dugout, Kunal walked like a ghost towards the coach, behaving like a shadow of who he actually was. He wanted to say something but decided not to. But the coach understood the feelings of his boy and said, "This is the exact time which will make a solo performer like you realize that cricket is a team sport and carrying water bottles for teammates is also a part of the game!"

"If you ever see me dangling from the top of a high-rise building, the only thing between me and certain death will be Canada Sir's outstretched hand," Kunal said to Ratandeep reconfirming his gratitude in the ideologies of his mentor.

It was a clinical performance by Monty's bowlers, especially Beta and Kalee and the opening batsmen were no match to them. Though the call of batting first on an overcast afternoon was a brave one, the clouds seemed to disappear with every passing over and batting became easier. Canada had kept the plan and techniques simple and therefore his boys were under no heightened pressure to perform. Perhaps that is why they not only seemed their happiest but also enjoyed playing and competing against the champion batsmen.

At the end of 15 overs, the scorecard read 92/4. They had been treading on water all this while but it was now a swim or sink situation for Officers XI. The batsman under pressure to hit a boundary surprisingly tried a reverse sweep on the first ball of the sixteenth over from Pappu. He missed the ball completely and it went on to rattle the middle of the off stump, handing the spinner his first wicket of the tournament. Instead of celebrating, the Brave Dogs quickly formed a huddle and Monty reminded them about the coach's bowling and the fielding strategy for the new and the most explosive batsman of the lineup, Hemant.

Canada fleetingly felt the heat of some of the most difficult emotions. For a crystal clear set of logical reasons, he wanted Hemant to do well but he could not afford the player to explode against the coach's own team. He was a like an isolated man sitting on the sand at the banks of a river only to observe it flowing, thinking that the water would unquestionably calm in a few days and so would he. There was nothing he could do apart from staying calm and watch his inexperienced men compete against his own favorite player. Cricket is neither immune from the society's wider issues nor from the individual thoughts of the players and coaches.

Hemant tried to loft the first ball he faced in the gap for a quick single but could not time it well enough. It rocketed up so high that most people in the crowd lost sight of it, but not Alpha, who was attentively fielding at long on. It was supposed to be a simple catch but perhaps the wind swirled away the ball and the fielder made a mess of it despite getting both hands on the leather. "Catches win you the matches," was exactly what Canada had explained to each of his players. That contrived drop not only resulted in two runs, but also gave another life to the hard hitting batsman.

Canada was proficient enough to know the exact feeling of Alpha and consequently gestured towards Monty to signal to him to not say anything inappropriate to the panic-stricken fielder. Though the catching practice was up to the mark, the poor guy was only a human and clearly did not spill it on purpose. Pappu was visibly a bit disappointed but confident at the same time as he could actually manage to make Hemant play a mistimed shot, something that most bowlers of Kanpur struggled to do. The next ball was a flipper, precisely what they had planned, and it followed the backing away batsman. He was cramped for room and hence once again did not get the timing right as he attempted to sweep it towards deep fine leg. The ball ballooned in the air and ended up in the safe hands of Beta Kumar fielding next to the umpire, at backward square leg. The younger brother did not repeat the mistake committed by the elder one.

Staring was not quite the word to describe the look that the batsman gave to the overjoyed bowler on is way out. His eyes did not blink but slowed and the effect was not soft and inviting but harsh, too harsh. The clear-cut and explosive mouth gave away all his intention as he departed saying, "I will be back with the ball in hand!"

Brave Dogs restricted Officers XI to a mere 116/9 in their quota of 20 overs, a score which many agreed was much below par, especially for the defending champions. However, they were equipped with the right kind of bowlers to defend it. In fact their bowling attack was the one which affected all out on the previous opposition for only 38 runs. They were definitely capable of dismissing even the strongest batting lineups below 100 runs.

"Beware of the bouncers!" said Canada as Sarfaraz and Dipshit padded up and then turned to his other batsmen. "We need to be smart to chase tricky totals like this one. Assume that the match is of 18 overs. Monty, the score is tailor made for your style of batting. We need at least one end secure till the sixteenth over and then take it onwards from there. Sooraj, you are batting at number five and Kamlesh will slog at four. Beta and Alpha are going to finish it for us with Junaid playing a supporting role to Monty and also the floater according to the situation."

"Sarfaraz, remember to use the pull shot I taught you for maximum impact," said the thirteenth man Kunal making sure that his replacement gets the best of the tips till the last moment.

Astonishingly, Sarfaraz successfully swiveled on the pull and got it between the deep fine and deep square for a four. It was indeed a slower bumper but the batsman did well to get in into the gap, thereby giving a positive start to the run chase. In the same over, Dipshit received a fuller delivery and he wristed the ball powerfully over long on for a six, taking the score to 12/0 after one over, a start that nobody in the stadium had imagined.

"Let us stamp our authority and take them out of the game as early as we can," said

Dipshit with a punch to the glove of Sarfaraz as the batsmen met in the middle of the pitch at the end of the over. As he was walking towards the crease to take strike, one of the fielders elbowed Sarfaraz in the stomach and jogged out of the personal space of the batsman, completely destroying his focus.

The dirty old trick worked. It was a seam up ball, full and angled in on the stumps. Though the young tailor tried to whack it across the line after clearing his front leg, he failed to make any contact. The ball beat the inner edge of the bat and the middle stump went flying into the air. The bigger percentage of the crowd had been waiting for that moment and naturally they erupted.

The moment they saw that the next batsman walking towards the crease was the Brave Dogs' captain, Monty, a few notorious ones screamed, "Scarlett is still alive!" and others joined. Some of them had brought with them three feet long posters of Scarlett while some had giant sized dummies of elongated cigarettes. They acted as though they were smoking them. Each member of the Brave Dogs camp including Beta seemed to be intolerant at the scornful, disrespectful, insulting and ridiculous act from the crowd. If a languorous smile is supposed to be an indication of acceptance, Officers XI seemed to like the unforeseen scene created by their fans.

On the other hand, the supporters of the red jersey had gone completely mute. Tara almost retreated inside of herself. Instead of watching the proceedings live, she watched it as if everything was playing on a screen. The sound of taunts, laughter and boos arrived into her ears from somewhere far away. She could not gather courage to take out of her bag the two feet long poster of Monty which she had carried with her all the way from her home. Even Pornika, Tanmey and Sweety had their brains disastrously shut down. They had no counters whatsoever to those types of provocative and cynical jibes.

Monty's own brain stuttered for a moment too. Though his face was half covered by the helmet, there were enough gaps for the noise to make its way to his ears and the visuals to form an image on his retina. He could feel strange warmth at the back of his neck and a slight tingling at the tip of his fingers but then he heard a distinctive voice of Canada, "Answer them!" Without turning back Monty took a very deep breath, raised his left arm and gestured a thumbs up towards his coach as well as to the people raising their voice to ridicule him. He even blew a kiss to a random person in the crowd who was carrying a poster of Scarlett White. Perhaps the kiss was actually directed to her. That body language and calm from the captain gave Tara the confidence to take Monty's poster out and wave it like a flag, though still lost somewhere in the chaos.

Though the bowler was a quickie, Monty charged out of the crease as if playing against a part time spinner, got to the pitch of the ball and whacked it over the wide long on for a mountainous six that landed on the second tier. If the shots could ever be compared to kings, that one was the lord. Not only did it change the dynamics of the match, it also changed the body language of the fielders. Their shoulders drooped and so did of their fans. That one shot was powerful enough to convert the noise to silence, dead silence.

At the end of the over, Monty used his hands to gesture towards the crowd, asking them to make some noise. This time, it was the turn of the people in red who found their lost voices back. Once again there was a kiss blown by him but not towards Scarlett's posters, but towards Tara, making her fall down on her own seat, unable to believe what just happened. Canada too responded with thumbs up from the dugout and then sat on a chair with his legs up. He turned towards his boys and said, "Keep calm as we are going into the semifinal."

The next few overs were all about steady consolidation and at the end of the power play, the scorecard read 58/1. The decidedly interesting hunt for runs turned more and more undemanding with every ball finding the middle of the bat of both batsmen. To change the equation, Hemant brought himself on and set one of the most aggressive fields, placing eight agile fielders into the ring with most of them in catching positions.

Perhaps it was more of a lapse of concentration for Monty than good bowling by

Hemant. The slower ball was much outside off but Monty tried to smash it towards the leg side, managing only to slice a dolly to the mid on fielder. "Extra cover would have been a sensible option," screamed Canada as he jumped out of his chair in agony. Hemant just opened the tiniest of the floodgates for the Officers XI and celebrated his counterpart's wicket with his trademark crucial wicket style, the one in which he ran like a crazy homicidal maniac towards the inner circle with both his arms raised high in air and fists clenched as tight as they could possibly be. If there were insects flying around, at least a dozen would have entered his open mouth, if only.

The situation directed Canada to promote the floater Junaid to number four. Singles, doubles and a couple of odd boundaries constituted a steady partnership between Dipshit and Junaid and moved the score to 100/2 in 14 overs when Dipshit mishit a juicy full toss, flat and straight into the bucket hands of the fielder at fine leg. In order to get the crowd going, he animatedly pointed at the bull dog printed at the middle of his t-shirt on his way back, a signal perhaps to Pornika and others not be disappointed. Surely the Brave Dogs were not going to lose it from there. Alpha too received a promotion as they attempted to finish the match clinically, but it was Junaid who scored the winning boundary, ironically of the bowling of Hemant.

The faces of the Officers XI fell faster than loaves of bread removed from the oven too soon. Their captain's bottom lip jutted out and his shoulders dropped much more than before. The scenes were totally opposite in the Brave Dogs' dugout. Though the inexperienced players did not run out to pick their buddies on shoulders, they simply patted on each others' backs and exchanged some hi fives. Nobody had imagined that the Brave Dogs could qualify for the semifinals after a comprehensive victory over the defending champions.

Though Canada was the eldest individual on the field, he stood near the boundary rope, hopping from one foot to the other like a little kid. He was deliriously happy, giddy even and of course, justifiably proud. Every few seconds he either punched the air around him or clapped his hands. He had realized the fact that his prediction, Hemant, would not be the one winning The Pride of t20 cricket trophy but that did not matter to him anymore. The irrepressible excitement of qualifying for the semifinal had momentarily compelled him to unconditionally forget about Shefali and her marriage.

Dipshit collected the man of the match award for his exquisite half century. Before marching towards the dressing room, the Brave Dogs got together in a huddle for their team anthem, with Canada shouting louder than anyone else, "You may think that we are the underdogs but no, no, no! We are the Brave Dogs, the mighty mighty Brave Dogs! Woof, woof, woof!"

15

MAD AND INSTINCTIVE FIGHT

Wednesday, 24/June/2020

At Shakuni Children's Park

"**A**nd last but not the least I warn you guys that all that the Challengers are good at is aggressive intimidation of their opponents through their unsophisticated actions and trashy words. Now that you know what they would try to do and why, I do not think you should care even a bit about it. Till today we were just answering the taunts aimed at us, but now we have earned the right to start the banter too! Do not forget to remind the Challengers that they are just a team with some big names in their lineup but never have they ever won any trophy," concluded Canada as the practice session came to an end. It was perhaps the shortest one with each batsman facing only a handful of balls and the bowlers not bowling more than a couple of overs. The main motive obviously was to finalize their game plans for the semifinal. After they were instructed to disperse, the players casually began to chat with each other.

"That's a brilliant watch!" said Dipshit as Ratandeep flaunted his new expensive smart watch in front of his colleagues. Almost everyone wanted to take a look at it and learn about its technological features. The proud owner mentioned the price around ten times as he probably wanted to make each of his teammate realize that he was significantly affluent.

Perhaps Kalee was the only one not interested and Ratandeep did not like that a bit. "Why do you not want to see my new watch?" he asked.

"As every poor man should, I know my limits. I am not interested in seeing anything that I know I cannot afford."

"I am not exhibiting it with the purpose of showing off!"

"Yes of course, rich men like you have nothing called attitude. All they have is a standard," said Kalee as his voice got louder.

"I repeat I am not showing off!"

"You neither have a handsome personality that can compliment this watch, nor do you have any recognizable talent to make it to the playing XI. It is only because of your hardworking father that you are rich and just like any other spoiled brat, you love to show off and perhaps even waste the money earned by him."

"Do you want a fistfight?" Unbridled anger had already boiled up into Ratandeep due to what he thought was a senseless conversation started by Kalee.

"If you want it, remember I am stronger than you."

What followed was so quick that nobody could see who threw the first punch but suddenly, Kalee's fist slammed into Ratandeep's face as the latter's spiked boot created a bloody mess on the former's left arm. They stumbled apart with the impact and after catching their breaths, they dived once again into each other with their eyes narrowed in determination. Before Ratandeep could break his opponent's nose with his elbow, the other players pulled both of them away from each other. The incident however resulted in a lot of intense and incoherent noise, reaching the ears of the coach and the captain who were busy discussing certain game plans, standing just twenty steps away.

Canada ran towards them, shouting, "What is wrong with you two?" Monty meanwhile joined his teammates. Pappu chronologically narrated what had happened in just one breath.

The players looked at Kalee, who was just standing normally as if nothing had happened. Canada saw the blood and said, "Thank God, it is not your bowling arm. Somebody, give him a clean cloth to tie around the wound." Junaid gave him his unused white handkerchief and Kalee wrapped it around his wound as tight as he could, to stop the blood flow.

Ratandeep was profoundly furious but he did not want to break anyone's bones. Almost choking and finding it difficult to breathe, he stormed out of the park without even saying a word to the coach or to any other player. Beta Kumar dared to stop him but he just pushed him aside on his way out. That push was so hard that Beta would have obviously fallen face first on the ground had Alpha not held his hand.

"The session is over for the day. We all will now meet at the stadium for the semifinal. Do not think much about this incident. We need to be positive. Kalee, you stay back, others can leave." And that was exactly what followed. Even Monty left with them. Perhaps he was as concerned about his good friend Ratandeep as that troubled person who forgot to clear his browsing history before lending his laptop to someone from his own family.

Though Canada wanted to literally slap Kalee for the unruly, unmannered behavior exhibited by him, the long and occasionally bitter experience that he possessed came to the rescue of his supremely resolute anger. He knew that vicious abusing and crazy shouting won't make any difference whatsoever to Kalee, so he opted for an improbable approach.

"Remember the teacher who generally overlooked your innocent silliness despite watching you closely at school? Your coach is like that teacher," said Canada looking straight into the eyes of one of his most incomprehensible player, trying to extract an unexpected reaction from him.

"But I have never been to school. I cannot even write my own name," Kalee answered back with his characteristic poker face and a gruff voice.

"Remember how patiently your parents watched you create a comical mess at home but never said a word against their beloved son? Your coach is like your parents."

"But I grew up as an orphan on the streets of Kanpur. Never have I ever seen the people who threw the newly born me behind a pile of stinking garbage and then ran away, hiding their faces in the dark hue of a cold night."

"Remember God is watching," the smile on the brown lips bloomed like a spring flower as Canada sensed that finally he would be able to preach something to his player. That sense clearly came from deep inside to light up his eyes and gradually spread into every part of him.

"But I do not know the religion of the people I was born to. Perhaps not by choice, but due to the lack of it, I grew up as an atheist. Though in my younger days, I opted to let people know my full name when I begged outside temples in the afternoon, I removed the K from it in the evenings when I begged near the mosques." A person smiles with his mouth. Kalee was different. Though there was no hint of any expression on his face, a double-edged smile could be heard in his voice, in the choice of his words and the way he relaxed.

Canada's natural smile faded into a fake one. In his opinion that was the best way to end the grueling session. Coming straight to the point, he said, "Be kind to others Kalee. It is not necessary to compliment them when in reality all you want to do is just the opposite, but at least be polite. When someone does not do well, don't try to show him down. We are one unit and that should leak through our body language, words and actions. I understand that each one of us is from a completely different background, but what I also know is that we are determined men having the same goal and that should be our motivation to win this tournament. If we have attitude problems within our squad, our mission would fail and all of us would end up being disappointed."

"Yes Sir. I have understood what you are trying to say. It won't be repeated," said Kalee. The shake of the head from the player was kind of a victory for Canada. He had successfully managed to reform a man who he considered to be the most inarticulate member of the squad.

16

SPOT FIXING

Thursday, 25/June/2020

"The day is not far when after losing me, you will miss, complain, cry for me and want to see me again," was the song that played at a bearable volume as Sooraj sat on the driver's seat of his dilapidated, rickety mini cab. Though the song was a tribute to unfaithful lovers, Sooraj wondered if it could be linked to money too. Once the money has been recklessly spent and there are limited sources to earn it back, the lines of the song are exactly what the imaginary cash would say to the pompous spendthrifts.

On the spur of that moment, a couple of young men opened the rear doors from either side of his cab and comfortably sat in it. Though the one wearing an odd rectangular pair of glasses had an extremely thick and unkempt beard, the other had a conservatively symmetrical one. Surprisingly, both of them were tall, well dressed and flamboyantly handsome.

"Sir, you need to book the cab using the mobile application," said the wicketkeeper without even bothering to look at his prospective clients.

"We are here to make you rich," said the man with glasses, sitting on the right side. His scratchy, monotonous voice compelled Sooraj to turn around in vivid but undefined anticipation.

"What is the deal?"

"Drive us to Kalee, the main bowler of your team." Though the face of the vigilant man on the left was flat and expressionless, his voice was sweet and agreeable. He opened the black, well-worn briefcase which he was carrying and showed Sooraj that it contained several piles of two thousand rupees currency notes, apart from a couple of signed blank cheques, a ball pen and a slim, broad, sharp meat chopper knife.

In that split second before the foul but sweet smell of the notes could make its way to the nerves in Sooraj's nose, his brain and also his body electrified. It was the stimulating expectancy of something that needed more words to express than he could ever think of. Without wasting any more time, he turned the key and began to steer the cab towards the slum where Kalee dwelled.

The impatient and perpetually cranky people on the dirty, appallingly rutted streets of the slum appeared capriciously cruel, especially with their eyes peeping inside the cab, probably because it was the only car in the locality at that time. The only splash of bright color in the brown was visible in the indecipherable and occasionally obscene graffiti that were present on most walls. There were some middle aged women in skimpy outfits and high boots looking for work, their bodies as thin as pins and their cheekbones jutting out through pale skin.

"This is the locality where Kalee works and lives but I do not know the exact location where we can meet him," said Sooraj as he parked his cab exactly in the middle of the narrow street.

"Ask that pan masala seller about him," said the spectacled man pointing towards a lone old man casually sitting in a bean bag sized pan shop.

Sooraj got down from the car to ask the old shopkeeper and some random people about Kalee's exact address; precisely following the most commonly used method before the technical invention of smartphone maps. He returned after gathering complete information.

"Take a left from here into the lane. He will definitely be visible somewhere there," he said to his two customers but they did not want to get down from the car and requested Sooraj to go, look for and bring Kalee with him. Sooraj was indeed a man who could do anything for money. Without a second thought, he walked into the narrow lane looking for his friend.

As he took steps one after the other, Sooraj felt himself almost in physical contact with the contiguous stretch of featureless yet towering walls on both sides. There were some wooden doors too and all of them opened inwards as there was no space for them to open towards the lane. He heard the familiar sound of water gushing from the sink, the dropping of utensils on the floor, the shriek of a drilling machine, the hammering of furniture, the sound of rough voices. So many people behind those walls but none in the little space on the front side where he was walking. The experience was revolting.

All of a sudden, a cold and moist hand came out of one of the doors and pulled him into a shoe store with an exceptionally limited collection of not more than a dozen pairs of sufficiently strong leather shoes for men. The ceiling was just six feet in height and for Sooraj, who was around six feet tall himself, it was impossible to stand straight. Surprisingly, he was pulled in by a twenty something stunning salesgirl dressed in an ironed half sleeved white shirt but nothing below it.

"Give me hundred rupees," she said in a low, shaky voice.

"I don't even know you," he replied with his unblinking eyes pointing straight at her dark long legs and surprisingly delicate bare feet.

"If you don't give me hundred rupees, my man will punch and break your nose for piercingly staring at me."

Sooraj did not want to create a scene. He took out a note of hundred rupees from the pocket of his shirt and said, "I will give this to you only if you tell me where Kalee stays."

All of a sudden she moved towards the door, her pleasantly youthful face creased and her fists closed so tight that she could perhaps feel the sweat trapped inside them.

Before Sooraj could understand what was going on, Kalee jumped down from a window like opening in the ceiling. All this while he was hiding in the place where the shoe stores keep a lot of stock and there always are some men positioned there to throw and catch some boxes when the customers reject certain footwear or want to try more options.

"What is going on here?" said Sooraj as his eyes now opened as wide as they could.

"Welcome to my house. I live and work here and this exploitative girl is my business cum live-in partner," replied Kalee with a reprehensible smile on his face. The bold girl smiled too.

"This is not the time to welcome me. It is the time to meet the two men waiting for you in my cab. They are here to make us rich."

Without even thinking or discussing about what they should or should not do, Kalee and Sooraj solemnly marched towards the cab leaving the salesgirl alone in the gloomy shoe store.

Under the instructions of the two men, Sooraj turned up all the glasses and locked the car as the private meeting between the four of them officially began.

"You both are playing for twenty thousand rupees only," said the glassed man, "but don't you think you deserve more than that? Look at some of the players playing for other teams. They get paid in lakhs. In fact Gorillas and Officers XI were two of the most expensive teams in terms of player fees, but what actually happened? You guys managed to beat them."

"We are not contracted players," pointed out Sooraj as he exchanged an eye contact with an over-thinking Kalee sitting adjacent to him on the co-driver's seat.

"How does it matter? Your coach is using you guys to lift the trophy. And it is not at all wrong to do so but at least he should pay the amount his players actually deserve."

"But we cannot go against Canada Sir," said Kalee as he tried to unlock the door, only to be stopped by Sooraj, who seemed much more interested in the conversation.

"Be patient. We are here for some mutual benefits. Kalee, you don't have to go against your team or your coach, you just have to bowl one extra delivery in the next match."

"Please elaborate," said Sooraj as Kalee was facing difficulty in registering the words that he just heard.

"Just make sure that the any one ball of your first over in the match against the Challengers is a front-foot no ball. That is all you need to do to earn one lakh rupees. Neither will it make a big difference to the result of the match, nor will anyone have any kind of doubt on you."

Kalee's mixed emotions told him that he needed a telepathic connection with his partner in crime Sooraj. His eyes had entered into a different state from what they used to be in. The professional cricket enthusiasm had perhaps been crushed to multiple pieces and conquered by an excessive desire for money. The deal sounded safe, uncatchable and lucrative. One no ball in the entire innings would never put him under the coach's efficient radar anyway.

"What will be my cut?" said the wicketkeeper Sooraj as he seemed desperate to bag a role for himself in the foul play.

"You are the most important person in the set up. Just before a no ball is about to be bowled, you will open your wicketkeeper's gloves, drop them flat on the ground and then wear them again. This will be a signal to us in the crowd that everything is going as per the plan. You get one lakh too for your uncomplicated and effortless action."

Though it did not suit his moustaches, Sooraj's face turned rosy in a blush. He peeped out through the glass of the car for a couple of breaths and then turned to his teammate, who was already looking with his observant but half closed eyes at the former. In that weird moment, a peculiar kind of unaided telepathy literally worked. Anticipatory smile blossomed on the two faces and they cautiously nodded.

"We are in!" they said together. Even if they were salted real pistachio nuts, they would have still sneezed saying, "Cashew!"

"If you take the money and do not act as instructed, then remember that we carry a double edged meat chopper knife at all times with us!" said the man on the left as he unlocked the briefcase with a mirthless smile taking over the crooked grin on his face.

"Cheque or cash?" asked the other one.

"Cash, we don't work for cheques ever!" both the Brave Dogs simultaneously replied without any discussion. Though they were not income tax payers, they were aware about the government bodies keeping a close eye on each bank transaction like a hungry lioness keeps track of her seemingly unsuspecting prey.

"See you at the stadium. Good luck for the match against the Challengers! Remember, we never met and do not know each other."

The complete payment was made in advance. The stupefying smell of under the table cash overpowered all other senses of the duo. The two innately bashful men left the cab after exchanging crisp bundles of brand new currency notes worth two lakhs. They had booked another cab from that location as they did not want Sooraj and Kalee to know or even guess the address of their underground den.

Easy money creates emotional indifference between people, replacing love, respect and gratitude. Not caring about the possible dangers of spot fixing, both the Brave Dogs giggled like little kids as they counted the notes in as much chaotic manner as humanly possible. Perhaps never in their life, had they seen such a big amount at one time. The micro interaction probably shaped their brain in a poor manner and successfully managed to decrease the empathy and creativity in their prefrontal cortex. There is never a good future without money and that is precisely what both of them were aware of. Money has the power to change anybody, anytime, anywhere.

17

THE CONTENTIOUS SEMIFINAL: BRAVE DOGS V CHALLENGERS

Sunday, 28/June/2020

People who woke up late on Sunday assumed that it was too early to be up as the natural light could hardly penetrate the fabric of their shelters. The air was humid and smelt of storms. Nobody realized when the dull, overcast morning turned into a darkened afternoon. A chink of light managed to break through the black clouds but was not enough for a game of cricket. There was no choice for the organizers but to get the floodlights switched on despite the fact that it was supposed to be a day affair. It was indeed as dark as pre-dawn.

For the Brave Dogs it was supposed to be a special day, their first semifinal. They did not complain about the various shades of grey in the sky and reached the stadium on time. Though they were bright eyed and bushy tailed in hope for a chance to play under the artificial lights for the first time ever in their short careers, the rapid excitement soon turned to an unusually vivid apprehension. Ratandeep did not turn up for the match. Perhaps his dramatic inability to fully recover from anger after the trifling quarrel with Kalee was the reason behind his absence.

"The conditions are dictating us to play an extra pacer today and irony is that he is the one missing," said Canada agonizingly as he walked away towards the washroom kicking the set of bails kept near the wooden bench in the dressing room. Not a single player dared to say a word as the facial expressions of the coach were no mask to his facile but intense aggression.

"Call Ratandeep," said Jaganbir and Kunal immediately called him but the fast bowler's mobile phone was switched off.

The entire squad appeared as much confused as the last bench students get with their chances of passing a difficult subject's examination. Behaving like a leading youth politician from a historical political party, Kamlesh wanted to call his mother to ask her the solution for the issue. Others somehow had still not lost their ability to think logically. They stopped him from doing so.

With less than ten minutes left for the toss, Monty and Canada mutually decided to go ahead with the spinner Pappu and struck off Ratandeep's name from the team's playing XI sheet that the captain had to submit to the match referee at the time of the toss.

"Remember guys, we do not have many substitute fielders. In fact, Kunal is the only one. So, I request you all to be extra careful while fielding," said Canada as Monty walked out for the coin toss.

"My name is Hosh Patel and I send my opponents to hospital," said the six and a half feet tall, ninety kilograms heavy captain of the pink jersey Challengers as he introduced himself in his typical Gujarati accent, followed by a wicked kind of laughter, similar to the one from the Rakshasa family in Ramayana.

Monty impudently smirked. It was just a small pout of the pristine lips and narrowing of the eyes followed by tilting of the head and the return of the favor, "The garbage will be picked up after three hours. Are you ready?"

Before Hosh could reply, the umpires requested him to toss the coin without any further delay. Heads it was and Monty lost the toss.

The moment Hosh opted to bowl first Monty knew that his batting line up was going to face an uphill task coping with the dangerous swing on offer due to the overcast conditions. He put on a fake smile, the one he had mastered over the last few months. Perhaps he thought that the challenge would be easier that way.

"The key is not to lose wickets. I do not care about the runs we score. The only thing which matters is that we need to bat out full 20 overs against the five pacers they have in their bowling lineup," explained Canada. He was certain that his boys knew that he was trying to hide the actual gravity of the demanding circumstances, but still he was determined to hide it.

The truth was nobody knew what to expect from the pitch until Sarfaraz took a savagely fierce blow to the helmet on the very first delivery of the innings. The doctor on duty tested him for concussion but ruled it out as the innings continued. Canada contorted his lips into an awkward, toothy smile but his cheeks behind the beard were not at all compromising. Somewhere deep down in his brain, he knew that the Brave Dogs' campaign was about to end soon.

Seeing a slower length ball, probably misfired by the bowler, Dipshit charged down the pitch, a move that Canada had strictly instructed him to avoid. The line meant that he had to fetch it from outside off stump and while doing so, he skewed it straight up towards mid on. Hosh never dropped those. "This pitch is not for moving the feet too much," shouted Canada as he raised and lowered his arms in slow motion and then stood still, grim faced.

Monty walked out, prepared mentally to play his natural game. Little did he know that Hosh was still looking forward to a revenge for the humiliation he had to face at the time of the toss. As he got ready to take strike, the wicketkeeper and the close in fielders turned their back towards the batsman and placed their palms over their noses. The bowler too did not begin his run up.

"What is wrong?" said the umpire to the Challengers' captain who was standing close to him.

"This batsman is a fart factory. Let the smell clear and then we will clear him up. He has a truck to catch in a couple of hours, the one going to the garbage dump," replied Hosh with his left hand still on his nose as he jogged back towards his fielding position.

When Monty averted his gaze away from the fielders, his face fell lifeless, allowing his eyeballs to get to an unusual cold hard gawk. All of a sudden the bowler began his run up and Monty had to play the first ball of his innings, not quite in the way he wanted to and hence edged it, luckily to no man's land.

The batting was indeed tough and required a high level of skill set to be applied. The bowling on display by the Challengers was sheer brilliance. Very rarely did they go off the radar. A large number of deliveries were pitched in the corridor of uncertainty and caused a lot of problems to the Brave Dogs' batsmen. At the end of 14 overs, the scorecard read 89/5 with Monty, Dipshit, Beta, Sarfaraz and Junaid back in the hut after playing some ordinary strokes.

Hosh brought on himself to bowl the fifteenth over with Alpha on strike. The first ball was a quick one that angled in off the pitch and the batsman was late on the glance. He got trapped right in front of the stumps. The Challengers began to celebrate the LBW but the umpire raised his left arm sideways signaling a no ball, thereby giving a life to Alpha. Hosh was obviously not impressed by the fair call. In order to release some of his frustration, he walked up to the batsman, looked straight into his helmet as if he was an enormous cannibal and said, "Your future girlfriend is my current match on the dating application!" The batsman did not respond, not because he did not want to, but because he had no answer.

On the free hit, Alpha Kumar went down flat on the ground like a bowling pin just struck by the heavy bowling ball but somehow managed to clear the fence. It possibly was one of the most outrageous shots ever. He knew that Hosh would try a yorker and thus, he almost sat. Even his eyes briefly closed but he somehow put bat to it and the connection was so good that it went over the wicketkeeper's head for a maximum. On his walk towards the starting point of his run up, Hosh was unexpectedly greeted by a mocking remark from the non striker Kamlesh. With a quirky smile on his face, he said, "Your future wife is his current Kundli match."

At the end of 18 overs, the scorecard meandered to 112/8 with Sooraj and Pappu battling it out at the crease. In an attempt to stop a boundary from the bat of Sooraj, one of the fielders twisted his ankle and on the advice of the physiotherapist, he had to go out of the field, injured. Canada termed the injury as a blessing in disguise for the Brave Dogs. The player who was out was actually the pacer who was deemed to bowl the last over. This clearly meant that the last over would be bowled by a part time spinner, a much needed advantage for the Brave Dogs. The score moved to 118/9 with Pappu departing on the last ball of the over, courtesy a magnificent throw from the deep to run him out.

Kalee walked out to bat in the last over. Though he was an unpredictable bowler, nobody knew what he would come up with a bat in his hand. Neither had he auditioned as a batsman, nor did he ever practice batting. Reaching the middle of the pitch, he punched in the glove of Sooraj as the two stood still waiting for the Challengers' mini conference to get over.

Meanwhile, Kalee spotted two familiar faces sitting together in the front row of the crowd and showed them to Sooraj too. Because of the weather forecast, only a handful of people had gathered to watch the game. Perhaps that was the reason why those two men were clearly visible from the pitch. They were indeed the men who had given one lakh rupees each to the two batsmen out there. While a deadly meat chopper knife was printed on one of their t-shirts, the other one had some bundles of currency notes printed on it along with a line that read, "Grab these to get rich!"

Sooraj worked the first delivery towards the onside for a single and that brought Kalee on strike for the first time ever in the tournament. What followed was both unpredictable and unbelievable. According to the buoyant coach Canada, the dream finish deserved to be named The Kalee show. Though the bowler did not bowl a single delivery where the batsman actually wanted him to, remarkable footwork and overwhelming power of the man moved the score to a defendable 149/9 at the end of 20 overs, courtesy five magically stupendous massive sixes in a row from the number 11.

"Beta will open the bowling with the man of the moment Kalee," said Canada as he drew the fielding plan on a sheet of paper with all his players listening to him carefully as they formed the customary team huddle around the coach. "The overcast conditions are a boon to Beta and Kalee's bowling style, make the most of it! Remember they will not attack if you can swing it the way you do. Jaganbir, you need to deliver the best slower ones and off cutters to bamboozle them. Pappu, Alpha and Kamlesh you three will not bowl in tandem as we need to pick wickets and not just check the flow of runs. Sooraj, be ready to take a catch on every delivery."

The first over from Beta was right on target. Though the Challengers did not lose any wicket, the batsman struggled to adjust to the line, length and the swing generated by the all rounder. The scorecard read 2/0. Observing the stance and feet movement of the two batsmen, Canada felt the need to bowl some cutters. He spontaneously changed the plan and the second over was made the responsibility of Jaganbir, who too did a decent job. The score moved to 8/0. Beta was at his best in the third over but conceded a couple of boundaries courtesy inner and outer edges, taking the score to 19/0 in three overs.

Resorting to the initial plan, Monty gave the ball to Kalee who slowly marked his run up to bowl his first and the innings' fourth over. The two crafty gentlemen in the crowd stood up from their seats and moved near the wide metal grill which acted as a divide between the third man fielder and the crowd. One of them was already on call with someone. The wicketkeeper Sooraj and the bowler Kalee chose to just look at each other for a couple of seconds as if they considered one another as an autonomous robot, not a human who was there to be interacted with. It was as if the some crucial words circulated in their minds but they could not afford to allow them to flow outward into the world.

The first two deliveries were identical yorkers but the right hand batsmen somehow managed to get the toe end of the bat on both occasions that enabled the ball to trickle down the leg side, resulting in a single of each of them.

Sooraj's nerves frayed to the quick. In his building anxiety, he constructed elaborate rationalizations for why everything would turn out alright, but still the nagging voice in the back of his mind spoke of nothing but doom ahead. He took off both the gloves from his hands, dropped them gently on the ground, then picked them and wore them again. The Brave Dogs were not quite able to understand but thought that he did so because of comfort issues. Canada crossed his arms in the dugout but did not lower his eyes a bit. The wicketkeeper's signal was clearly visible to the two gentlemen. The one on call raised his right arm in anticipation of the no ball. Lakhs of rupees were laid on numerous illegal yet hopeful bets within the short time period between the second and the third balls of that over.

The batsman walked down the pitch and drilled the full toss from Kalee but straight to cover. Though it was an ordinary dot ball, some of the eyes turned to the umpire who heedlessly stood at his place in the posture of an inflated synthetic mannequin. Lakhs of rupees were lost, or perhaps won by some innocent chaps as Kalee did not bowl a no ball despite Sooraj's action.

The bowler knew how to keep a poker face. All those days spent on street sides, gambling and fooling others paid off after all. He appeared nonchalant. There was no sign of redness in his cheeks to betray him. Sooraj on the other hand felt a bit relaxed. There was a feeling in his gut that said, "No," but there was another in his heart that said, "Yes." He closed his eyes, turned his head up and thanked God for whatever happened.

"What is the role a sportsman can play if not to fight to find the courage to do what is right for his team? People might call it apprehensive but at the end of the day, how does it matter what people call? When a champion opts for bravery instead of being a puppet of fear, good things get inevitable," said Canada to Kunal in the dugout. And then he continued, "Kalee and Sooraj were offered one lakh rupees each to bowl a no ball. The first thing they did was to inform me about it. I told them to do what their souls direct them to do. They passed their character test today with flying colors!"

"But Sooraj dropped his gloves," replied Kunal with his mouth refusing to close due to the shocking revelation by the coach.

"He has a family to cater – two kids and a wife. No bookie can question his intentions now as he played his part perfectly. The entire blame falls upon Kalee who is certain that come what may, those two seemingly dull criminals cannot harm him. They surely can enter his locality with the idiotic motive to attack him, but if they choose to do so, even they know deep inside that what would return will not be their bodies but their news!"

"But why did they accept the offer in the first place?" Kunal curiously questioned as Kalee steamed in to bowl the last ball of his over with the scorecard reading 24/0 in 3.5 overs.

"Who says no to easy money? By the way, Kalee told me that because of this one lakh, his dream of taking *Baraat* with lots of music, dance, pomp and celebration to marry his girlfriend will be fulfilled."

Some call laughing as a noise that comes from the mouth, but when Kunal laughed, it was nothing like that. In fact, the laugh was in his eyes, in the way his face changed into that vision of relaxed joy, joy for his teammate's celebrations.

As Jaganbir returned to the attack to bowl the fifth over, Kalee went near the grill to field. Perhaps the fear of facing ruination converted into hot burning anger in the eyes of the two men near that grill. No sooner did they shout a couple of abusive words to Kalee, the Brave Dog turned around to wave at them with a smile showing gratitude instead of rage. When there is something senseless going on around a person, the primitive part of his brain gets activated to produce aggression. As one of the men pushed the grill with all his force, probably in an attempt to break it, the webbing of his own finger split open and a stream of red blood gushed out.

"Who are you guys and why are you pushing the grill? By the way I like the meat chopper knife on your t-shirt. It reminds me of the smallest one my neighbor uses at his meat shop," said Kalee, refusing to even identify them. Such is the power of cash, especially when exchanged without a receipt.

"We have not swirled a punch yet and already see you quiver," screamed the cash t-shirt guy but Kalee responded with another wave and that got the crowd seated behind the bookies going. Most of them obviously thought that the player was waving at them and began to enjoy the six hitter's fielding.

Meanwhile three of the police officers on duty ran towards the abusive corner of the stand and evacuated the two misbehaving spectators. They even apologized to the player for the willful misconduct of the unruly members of the crowd. Kalee nodded and continued to field casually, as if nothing out of the ordinary had ever happened.

The three deliveries from Jaganbir were interchangeable off cutters and resulted in 1, 2 and 1 runs respectively. A slight loose grip was used by the bowler on the fourth attempt and that helped the ball wobble in the air before shaping back cunningly to smash the top of off. As the new batsman walked to the middle, rain conjured a sweet pattern upon the Brave Dogs' skin, and suddenly hundreds of liquid globes began to reflect the greenery of the ground's grass. Though rain may be a cooling phenomenon on the warm summer days, it is always unwelcomed on a cricket pitch.

However it was not that heavy and the umpires decided to continue with the fifth ball of the over being a dot ball. All of a sudden water began to wash over the skin of the players, umpires and the spectators so strongly that they were compelled to feel as if they were standing in the flow of a river rather than a cricket stadium. And the only thing the players and umpires could do was to jog off to the shelters, allowing the active grounds' men to cover not only the 22 yards but much beyond that. In fact it took them only ten minutes to cover the entire playing area. The rain was there to stay and each player knew that.

Meanwhile, the Brave Dogs marched into their dressing room. On the way, Kunal praised Kalee for his brave decision of not bowling the no ball. Pointing towards the coach Canada Singh, Kalee replied, "That man is a father like figure for me. He has taught me how to bowl and how to work in a team. What he did not teach me is to betray my own people." And they joined others in the dressing room where Canada was doing all the talking.

"If the rain does not stop, the Challengers qualify for the final due to the fact that they have hit more boundaries than us in the previous matches," said the coach with a worried expression on his face and his arms bent forward.

"And if it stops, we will surely lose some overs, and that means each bowlers' quota will be of two or three overs instead of four. This also implies that we have already bowled out our main bowlers and will now have to bowl spinners," said Monty adding fuel to fire.

Several hours passed and the rain finally stopped. The grounds' staff was busy in preparing the ground for some action, if at all. The truck to collect garbage had already arrived and its driver was requested to wait by Hosh and Mr. Mishra, the head coach of the Challengers. Perhaps they had planned to humiliate the losing team by asking them to leave the stadium in that truck.

The umpires called both the coaches to the match referee's room where they opened the infamous Duckworth-Lewis Stern method calculation book. One of the umpires, informed the coaches, "We have thoroughly inspected the ground and the pitch. Though the outfield can be termed as dangerous because of the numerous water logged patches, we cannot deny that this is the all important semifinal. Thus, we have decided to have a five over innings. Since 4.5 overs have already been bowled, the Brave Dogs will have to bowl one more ball to legally constitute the match. Due to the fact that the Challengers have lost one wicket, the revised target now is 38."

"38!" shouted Mr. Mishra with his hairy arms raised high in the air and then he tried to look at every corner of the room at once. Though his anger was sympathetic and righteous, it subconsciously turned insane. Generating as much power as he could, he slammed the door on his exit saying, "That means we need 7 runs from one delivery!"

"A six can take the match to super over," explained the umpires as Canada came out delighted from the match referee's room, his face resembling that of a war hero on his return after inflicting an unfortunate defeat on one of the deadliest enemies.

"Fortune favors the brave!" said the coach as all the Brave Dogs circled around him for the last minute instructions. "Jaganbir, you just need to bowl in an area that makes it difficult for the batsman to fetch. Bowl wide of off stump. At worse he can take four runs of the edge. Remember anything would do but not a six!"

Monty set a 7-2 off side field for the final delivery. Though the move would certainly be criticized by most cricket experts, the Brave Dogs did not mind letting the batsman know the line where Jaganbir would bowl. They decided to pitch it in the good length area so that there is no chance even for an outer edge to fly over the head of Sooraj for a six.

All the reasons not to be anxious in such a demanding situation came flooding in the mind of Jaganbir as he started his run up. He could feel a soft panic as the air whizzed past his ears and those distasteful thoughts swirled into a vortex of stupidity as he reached the bowling crease. The result was that he could neither control the length nor the line of the ball and bowled a crazy wild wide, not just because of the line but also because of its height. Sooraj jumped as high he could to stop it from running away to the boundary but the ball deflected off his glove. Going against the physical principles of the team, Dipshit ran as fast as he could from the third man region and in an attempt to dive on the dangerous outfield, landed shoulder first on the ground. Though he tried to be back on his feet, he could not. Clutching his shoulder, he cried for help and the Challengers' doctor was quick to reach him for medical aid. Worse though was the outcome of the delivery – five wides.

2 from 1 sounded much better than 7 from 1 with 9 wickets in hand! Dipshit was carried on a stretcher outside the playing area for better monitoring and Kunal replaced him on the field, without even warming up before the challenge. Jaganbir was still on his haunches, hiding his face with both his hands, perhaps unable to believe what just happened. The other Brave Dogs were speechless and stood completely motionless at their respective fielding positions. The only one heard shouting some of the meanest Punjabi abuses was Canada, who perhaps literally wanted to slap his bowler but somehow controlled himself from entering into the playing area.

The match had to be completed. Jaganbir ran in to re-bowl the last ball. The premeditating batsman quickly moved towards the off stump and drove the ordinary length ball towards Monty at mid off. While the striker was half way down the pitch, the non-striker was caught ball watching. By the time he could reach the crease to complete the run, Monty gathered the ball and threw it towards the keeper's end. The direct hit broke the sticks with the batsman well short of his ground.

The celebration began with Canada Singh dancing like he had forgotten how to stand still. Monty moved his limbs like they were made of spaghetti, while Jaganbir's face was an epic picture of pure relief. Sarfaraz and Junaid's eyes ate up the scene like a post

Ramadan feast. Man of the match Kalee and the bench warmer Kunal felt supercharged and jumped till their heads were giddy. Dipshit was happy too but in a lot of pain. He was taken by the doctors to a nearby hospital for a scan.

Hosh Patel and his team left the stadium in haste, perhaps their minds still in denial of the fact that they had been eliminated from the 2020 edition of tournament. With them, the garbage truck left the stadium too with its driver cursing Mr. Mishra for wasting his precious time.

18

THE INEVITABLE CONVERSATION

Saturday, 05/July/2020

Evening before the final

It was almost 7PM when the sun sank lower in the sky, making the air cooler by approximately one degree Celsius. Various colors subdued in the fading light as it was already in the leisurely process of turning into the gloom of another sleepless night. The sharp shadow of the cement cricket bat and also the ball had already disappeared into the dark of the roof but Jamal aunty was still at her window trying hard to hear all the noise from her neighbor's house.

"When I was of her age, I never thought about making a boyfriend. In those days, girls never ventured into such scandalous and shameful acts," screamed Silky who was standing near the open door of Shefali's room.

Then she turned with incessant hostility towards Canada, who was standing next to her, not like a king but like a bishop placed adjacent to his queen on the chessboard. He sighed spiritlessly through a dumb pout as if inflating an unmanageable balloon as she continued, "Your extraordinary leniency and pampering has spoiled her. Mrs. Sharma's daughter was absolutely pure till her wedding night."

Canada opened his mouth to say something but chose not to say it. He could feel the heat rising to his cheeks and prayed it was not noticeable. He coughed like a sick man and then somehow made an absurd hand gesture, almost pleading Silky to stop the intense rebuking.

"Give her a new mobile every year. Latest model is a must for the most modern girl in our society," she continued after ignoring her husband's hand gesture.

In her favorite black dress, Shefali sat on her bed, silent, stock-still and categorically inscrutable, as if she was the human model for an artist painting an ambitious portrait. Next to her was the closed paperback copy of the novel that she was supposedly reading. Though she had been hearing such rude and unbearable remarks every day since her birthday, she never answered back. Her eyes were lowered, perhaps because of the fact that she still had no courage to look into the eyes of her own parents. Apart from surrendering her mobile to them, she had also completely cut off all kinds of contact with Zorawar.

"Not even once has this girl apologized. She thinks that her parents are her enemies," Silky continued as Canada walked slowly towards the staircase.

"Where are you going?" she was infuriated with Canada. "Chatt," her left hand struck her own forehead with the centre of the palm striking it perceptibly hard. "I had dropped water exactly at the point where you are standing now. I told you not to walk there. Look at yourself trying your best to spread water to all parts of the house. Don't you know that the cleaning maid comes only in the morning, or do you consider me a maid too? Do you want me to wipe the entire floor now? Fire the maid. I will do the wiping also from today."

As Silky proceeded towards the storeroom to grab a bucket and a wiper, Canada tried to stop her. "It will evaporate. No need to wipe," he said but obviously, she did not listen. In fact, the volume of her voice increased by several decibels and that prevented Jamal aunty from moving even an inch away from her window.

"Shut up. I am a maid, the maid who works for 24 hours a day, 7 days a week and 365 days a year. I will wipe the entire floor first and then cook food for you. Meanwhile, you go down and have whiskey. Let your loving daughter relax on her cozy bed like a princess and read the same novel again and again. Go from here. Prepare your beloved players for the match. Go."

With the final to be played the next day, Canada did not want to increase his blood pressure or fall sick that night. He knew that anger is an emotion that is often associated with a range of minor irritation to intense rage. He decided to end the conversation there and then. "No need to cook for me today. I am going to eat out. I will be back by 11PM. Goodbye," he said as he ran down the stairs and quickly walked out of the house in room slippers.

Still full of anger, Silky went to the bathroom to fill water in the bucket. As she bent to lift the heavy bucket up, she heard the faint sound of someone's footsteps right behind her. She knew that Princess Shefali would never come to help her wipe the floor. Her eyes began to wander and blinked more than usual as her body slouched, occupying lesser space than it normally would. Making up her mind to attack the intruder with the wiper, she turned around only to be extraordinarily stunned.

Shefali had already wiped the floor using a ragged cloth and had come there to dump it in the bucket. She was still poker faced but her mother, being a mother, realized that she wanted to talk. As she turned back to leave the bathroom, Silky said in a normal tone, "Shefali, come here."

Shefali's eyes glimmered with watery tears and she dropped down on her knees with her mother observing her carefully from a distance. She sobbed and tears flooded like water rushing down from a dam that had just broken down. The only time she stopped was to fill her lungs with fresh air. As Silky watched her daughter shake with grief and her tears flowing unchecked, there was a part of her breaking too. If Shefali was not the same, then neither would she be. "Come to the room," she said and Shefali inevitably followed her. Both of them sat next to each other for a much awaited conversation.

"Mom, I love Zorawar and he loves me too," Shefali started to speak her heart out. Her sobbing stopped but not her tears.

"I know that. Even your father knows that," replied Silky looking straight into the red eyes of Shefali.

"We are in a relationship since three years and wanted to tell you but due to dad's case we decided to postpone it."

"I know that and I even know that Zorawar has come several times to meet you here in your room. But, what you don't know is that every time he came, your dad saw him either hanging on the pipeline or hiding in the balcony. Do you think your parents are blind? Do you think your parents will not know a thing unless you tell them about it? Do we have a dozen off springs that it would be a headache for us to monitor each of them?"

Shefali's facial expression could be compared to that of a patient in coma lying on a hospital bed. Even a blank sheet of A4 sized paper had more things to express than her at that soul stirring moment.

Without taking her eyes off her daughter, Silky continued, "Zorawar is a good guy. Your father has praised him several times. Though I have never spoken to that boy personally, I blindly trust your father."

"If dad likes him, then why did he create such a disquieting situation?"

"In future, when you become a mother and catch your own unmarried off spring red handed in a compromising position, do not forget to tell me how you reacted."

"I am sorry," said Shefali pulling both her ears and trying in vain to check the flow of tears from her eyes. Moans escaped her lips through the suppressed sound of hiccups. Not just the salt but also the sugar of her soul poured out of her eyes. The sound of wailing and suffering echoed throughout the house. Perhaps it even reached Jamal aunty's window.

"Had you told us about this relationship, we would have talked to Zorawar's parents a long time ago. Now, the circumstances have changed. What if Jamal aunty or any relative of ours saw you in Lovers' lane with Zorawar that evening instead of your own dad? Though he was in impassioned rage at that time, your dad has for real set a couple of conditions for your marriage. I cannot blame him for doing so. Rage leads to the wrong side of the brain taking charge. Now, his ego is in the way. He cannot take back his words and I am sure you would not like him to do so either."

"I love dad a lot and do not want him to take his words back, but what about Zorawar? Can you imagine how much pressure he would be in to play well individually and also to make sure that his team wins?”

“Champions are those who play their best under pressure. Without pressure, even the average players can perform. His team has made it to the final courtesy the three consecutive unbeaten centuries from him. Even if he fails in the final, he is certainly one of the strongest contenders for The Pride of t20 cricket trophy.”

“But, can Southern Blasters defeat Brave Dogs? They have never won a final.”

“Brave Dogs have never competed in a final!”

“What does dad think about this match?”

“You know your dad, don’t you? You know that he has taken the name of ICC more number of times than he took my name in the last ten years. 2020 is the tenth year in a row when he is dreaming to win this tournament. Every year he makes it to the final and the records are 9-0 against him. This final is special for him as the team he is currently associated with plays against the team he coached for seven years before this. Basically, all 22 players on the field are going to be the ones trained by him. Still, the odds to lift the trophy are totally against him.”

“But Brave Dogs are rookies. Will they be able to put a stellar show against the experienced Southern Blasters?”

"Do not forget that even Zorawar was a rookie too when Canada first spotted him at the trials seven years ago."

"There are times when retreat from a war is termed as bravery, not cowardice. It takes a considerable amount of courage to backtrack, to let the enemy walk over, and to ultimately find another route around to eventual victory," quoted Shefali from her favorite novel The Selfish Betrayals by Abhishek Kapoor, and then added, "Sadness is my enemy. I have been sad for a long time but not anymore. Confusion was actually a wrong path I had taken but it is time for me now to backtrack. Let the gloom of the build up to the final walk over till I ultimately find another route to eventual happiness."

Silky stood up and in a moment her arms squeezed a fraction tighter around Shefali as she breathed more slowly. Her body melted into her mom's as every muscle lost its tension to the purified air of the room.

"Remember your dad loves you the most. He slapped Zorawar that night even when the first thought in his blazing mind was that it was your mistake and not his," Silky said as the two bodies separated after the warm hug.

"The stories that actually grab all the attention are the ones that do not involve accidents but people doing things on purpose," once again Shefali quoted from The Selfish Betrayals. "I will be at the stadium tomorrow for the match. The night is long enough to decide my purpose."

"Dinner will be ready in thirty minutes. Do not forget to carry a purse with you to the stadium and in that keep an extra pad as tomorrow is your second day," said Silky with a concerned look on her face as she reached the door to walk out of the room.

"Don't worry mom, I will carry a big leather bag with me tomorrow!"

19

EXCHANGE OF FAVORS

Sunday, 06/July/2020

Night before the final

Combined with the *poojas* and prayers, the Purnima fasts kept by numerous devotees the day before helped bestow happiness and prosperity to the city as the glorious white moonlight splashed down its watery glow onto Kanpur. Probably intentional, the power failure at 1AM tried its best to maintain viscous darkness all over but the fact that it was almost a full moon, helped bathe most manmade structures in magnificent illumination. Even some of the existing trees were silhouetted against the deep velvety sky.

The Almighty may never burden a soul beyond it can bear, and if He does, He is the one who makes sure that the soul gets an option to escape the serious challenges by uninterrupted sleeping. If calm had a definition, it had to be the thing diffused in the air between the walls of Monty's bedroom. In his dreams, he heard the loud chorus of his team, the cheerful sound of his boys laughing, singing and celebrating their victory in the final. Though he was asleep, he was awake in his soul, living the perfect moments of the future.

Just as he forcefully tried to change the wallpaper of Beta Kumar's mobile from Shefali's social media profile picture to the Brave Dogs' team picture with the trophy, there was a jarringly painful noise of the door bell that entered his body through the ear canal and did not make its way out until he opened his eyes.

In a couple of seconds, Monty funneled all his strength into his feet in order to use it to walk out of the bedroom and towards the main door, with his mouth shut and hands relaxed. On the way, he slammed his right little toe against his own bed. Though he always loved and praised the softness of his bed, that slam against its hard wood forced his mouth to utter an utterly offensive word. If only the bed had emotions, it would surely be somberly annoyed.

Peeping through the hole in the door would have made little sense because it was darker outside than inside. As Monty opened the door, his brain stuttered for a moment while his eyes tried their best to take in some light, a natural activity that could not be possible, courtesy the electricity corporation. Every part of him went on a pause, perhaps to catch up some strange and bleak thoughts.

The enticing woman struggling to keep balance in the dark had brought with her a harsh scent of alcohol. Though she seemed to make an effort to look normal, her head shook from side to side as if there was formidable tension in her and it had to be released like a whistling pressure cooker letting out steam. Though the pencil heels added at least four inches to her height, her short hair helped take a couple of inches off it. Dressed in solid denim blue shorts and a casual sleeveless grey open shoulder top carefully displaying her delectable navel, Tara appeared to have come straight from a nightclub.

CCTVs were connected to the inverter. Monty was no stranger to the fact that CCTVs have infrared night vision. He quickly pulled her in and locked the door before the sleeping guards could wake up and have an opportunity to watch live on cam a girl in skimpy outfit enter his flat late at night. If that happened, it would have surely given an overdramatized topic to the neighborhood families for their breakfast discussion.

The fact that Tara's hot coral lipstick still had as much shine as it must have had when she left her own home, was an indication of her transparent yet strong character. She felt pretty, witty and cool and it was evident from the way she carried herself. As Monty switched on the flashlight of his mobile, she pulled her shorts a little lower and her chest out just a bit, and said, "Where is the washroom?"

Monty guided her towards the washroom and even offered his mobile so that she could see where the pot was and where the sink was. After a couple of minutes, she came out. Getting rid of her heels next to the kitchen door, she headed barefoot towards the cozy bedroom.

"What is going on here?" asked Monty as he followed the guest to the unlighted bedroom.

"I love you Monty," she said as she made herself comfortable on the soft bed.

"You are drunk." Monty momentarily remembered his old days when he was handsomely paid by frustrated men for staging such scenes with their women to catch them red handed.

"Monty, I am here to request you something." Though she was drunk, untypically her voice had not deteriorated a bit.

"What?"

"Please lose tomorrow's match."

"You are drunk," he repeated.

"I request you," she said as she invaded his private space and wrapped her arms around Monty's shirtless body. She then rested her head on his chest and continued, "Shefali is my best friend since we were little girls who played with dolls. She always married her doll to the guy whom the doll loved, not the one chosen by its father."

Monty drew closer to Tara and that raised her heart rate from 65 to 100bpm. He even turned off the flashlight, making the bedroom pitch black. Tara had always prayed for the moment when Monty kisses her. It was a matter of seconds when her crush would leap into some kind of relationship. Her eyes closed, head tilted upward until she felt his lips, on her cheek. It was a peck as one would expect from an affectionate friend. She was crushed on the inside. That was how Monty saw her always, like a beloved, sweetest friend.

"I completely understand your concern and what your best friend is going through, but these emotions do not allow me to betray my own team. I cannot even think of losing a cricket match on purpose. Since the first day, the Brave Dogs have been trained to win the trophy. As a captain, my role is to lead my boys from the front. I am sorry, I cannot go ahead with your request," Monty said as clearly as he could and placed a couple of extra pillows between Tara and him.

She sobbed into his chest unceasingly, hands clutching at his shoulders. In order to console her, he said, "In my opinion, Shefali has the right to choose her own husband. After winning the trophy, I will talk to Canada Sir regarding this unpractical decision of his." A tiny lapse in the slow rocking from Monty, let Tara pull away blinking her lashes that were heavy with tears. She collapsed again, her howls worsening until she fell asleep on his chest.

She woke at 4AM and looked at Monty sleeping next to her. The electrical power had been restored and the dim 0.5Watt LED night bulb was on. Obviously he looked handsome even as he slept, that steady heart, those steady breaths, more than enough to make any innocent girl fall in love with him again and again. Tara was no exception. She demolished the boundary wall by removing the pillows and throwing them on the floor and shifted closer to him. With a touch as gentle as a bird's feather tickle, she caressed his face for a minute and then planted a kiss on his cheek whispering to the sleeping soul, "I still love you!" After leaving a distinct mark of the lipstick on his right cheek, she slept again.

Upon waking for the second time, Tara burrowed herself into the warm, soft sheet and rubbed the remainders of the sleep from her eyes. As she gazed out, her hand reached for her mobile. After going through the numerous notifications, she saw the time. It was 11:50AM. Her eyebrows curved upwards forming wrinkles in the forehead and the whites of the eyes became visible through eye widening when she saw that Monty was not in the room. Her jaw became slack and opened when she heard another woman's carefree voice, "Good morning!"

Rita was busy dusting the plastic stool next to the bed.

"Where is Monty?" asked Tara, pushing the lacy strap of her bra inside the top.

"He has gone to the stadium for the final match," replied Rita with a peculiar smile that forced Tara to check the button of her shorts.

"Why did not you wake me up?" she questioned as she sat cross legged on the bed and diagonally wrapped her own arms around her, pressing the bare shoulders gently with her palms.

"He told not to. You are a lucky girl. He never invites any female home." Even Rita's breath turned a bit rapid and urgent to match that of Tara.

"My parents are out of town, so I came here," cooked up Tara as she checked the lipstick and makeup she wore in the mirror opposite to the bed.

"You are not going to watch the final?" asked Rita as she hurriedly folded Tara's sheet.

"I do not have the stamina to watch it."

Though Tara carefully scrutinized her body, her makeup, her clothes and her sense several times, fortunately, everything was well intact.

20
THE FINAL:
BRAVE DOGS V SOUTHERN BLASTERS

Sunday, 06/July/2020

"**W**hat?" exclaimed Monty as Kalee revealed that the bone of his already injured left forearm had cracked after receiving direct impact of the rough, gnarled wooden baton from a policeman while protesting against a new Government policy. There was a pin drop silence in the dressing room just like there is in a school's classroom for a few minutes after the teacher compares it to a fish market.

"The new policy is for the benefit of the homeless. In the first place, why did you protest against it in such a violent manner?"

"The opposition party workers and some wannabe politicians offered me a thousand rupees. I could not say no," said Kalee. Though he tried to keep his usual poker face mode on, there was a hint of pain in his expressions as he checked the black colored splint for the third time.

"Now you have spent fifteen hundred on the doctor's fees and the splint," pointed out Sooraj, who was righteously annoyed.

"I protested against it too," scratching his oiled hair around the *choti*, Kamlesh joined the conversation too, "but I simply shared a post on social media. Thank God there are no baton charges online."

"The day people will realize how social media is used as an alternative to paid media for effective propaganda, you will be bombarded online," said Jaganbir who was busy in applying gel to prevent his hair from flying like those of the female model from a popular shampoo advertisement.

"The bigger issue is that we have already lost our top batsman Dipshit to injury and now our top bowler is not going to play. There is still no news of Ratandeep. This clearly implies that when Monty will walk out to the toss and declare that we are just ten players strong, the match will be called off and Southern Blasters will be awarded the trophy." Kunal was spot on. Beta coughed thrice, not because it came naturally, but because Kalee was declared the best bowler in the squad.

"Brave Dogs, how is the energy?" For some reason, Canada did not sound like himself as he entered through the open door of the dressing room with both his hands resting on his bloated paunch. Even before the captain could say a sentence, the coach raised his nose and furrowed his eyebrows together forming at least four wrinkles on his broad forehead. He was certainly in severe abdominal pain and rushed immediately to the washroom, leaving the players guessing.

"Nature's call I think," presumed Pappu as he tossed the practice ball up only to catch it safely.

Ten minutes passed, and then twenty and finally Canada came out. The left side of his faint red lip tugged upwards creating a sinister smirk on his otherwise serious face. He said, "I will never eat the waterballs of Gulgule again!"

"Sir, you should have asked me for a recommendation. Gulgule is an unhygienic man," said Alpha, with his eyes showing the kind of gentle concern a grandmother would have for her grandchild.

"Yes, I have heard several people suffer from acute food poisoning after eating Gulgule's stuff," said Dipshit, laying his right hand lightly on the shoulder of Alpha for support as he stood up.

"I think that Chat Corner is the best," Jaganbir too chipped in, feeling much more confident after the gel was successful in holding his hair.

"Is that where you go with Sweety?" asked Junaid tilting his face upwards to see Jaganbir's reaction. The intention behind his perking lips was not something that could easily be ensured.

"Shut up!" screamed Kunal. Though he was himself interested in knowing about Sweety's hangout joints, the vice captain in him was mature enough to understand the need of the hour. Reducing his volume a little bit, he continued, "Is this the right time to debate on the taste of waterballs served by various eateries? With less than five minutes to go for the toss, we need to put in the eleventh name on the playing XI sheet."

Kunal was yet to complete his speech when Canada once again ran into the washroom, leaving the former's system flooded with adrenaline, pumping and beating as if trying to escape.

"Go ahead with ten. We are one short but we cannot help it," said Sooraj as Monty was about to walk out of the dressing room for the toss.

Everything and everyone except Kunal showed that they would manage it but the fact that the coach's opinion was missing, made Monty a little bit apprehensive. Just as he kept his left leg out of the door, he heard a familiar voice from behind, "The eleventh name is Ratandeep Lamba."

The Brave Dogs found a new level of kinetic energy as they jumped for joy and gathered around their permanent bench player in an attempt to cheer him up for his dramatic debut. When a fresh investor mints money for the first time at the stock market, he gets intricate happiness. But, that happiness is always temporary and ends as soon as he starts losing even the principal. Ratandeep's anger was like that short term happiness.

Though it lasted for a day or two more than it should have, it had completely waned. In fact, he went on to pat the back of Kalee, wishing him a quick recovery.

"Guys, be safe, Herpes is contagious," said Monty as he walked out for the toss with unassailable confidence leaking out from the two gemstones of Onyx.

Monty had expected excitement, fanatically loyal fans and a perfectly manicured turf around the batting friendly 22 yards, but what he saw out of the dressing room was much beyond his slender presumptions. Not only were there close to three thousand people in the crowd, there were also a couple of nine feet wide stages built for the cheerleaders adjacent to the dugout of each team. The cheerleaders were already there, trying hard to entertain but most members of the crowd seemed resentfully disappointed, perhaps even ludicrously humiliated. Most of them teamed up to curse the arrangement by Hargurjeet Singh, shouting as loud as they possibly could.

Cheerleading had been a part of the ICC since its start. Never had thickly bearded men been assigned pompoms to cheer any team or to get the crowd going. All three men in red vest and white shorts had long beards and short hair. They carried multi-colored pompoms and posters displaying a sexist tagline from a popular two wheeler's advertisement. Similar posters were in possession of the yellow brigade too, though their hair were long and beards short. The only thing common in both factions, apart from their black beard, was that each one of them had abundant underarm hair, clearly visible as they raised their hands to display their fluffy pompoms.

"This is what happens after a noble man gets married. Anjana, you spoilt the fun," said Monty to himself as he walked towards the boundary line, observing that around 5% of the fans, including Tanmey, Pornika and Sweety were actually in red supporting Brave Dogs. That was a moral victory in itself.

The visual of a fair complexioned girl with long and untied black hair appealed the most to Monty's unblinking eyes. Dressed in a round neck yellow top which clearly indicated that she was there to support Southern Blasters, surprisingly the girl was sitting with the red team supporters. After a sufficiently swift investigator's observation, he realized that she was indeed Shefali. "The father lost against the boyfriend!" and "Brave Dogs – 0, Southern Blasters – 1," were the exact phrases that bounced inside his skull in a loop, unable to find a release point till he reached the middle of the ground.

They say that a blank expression implies lack of strong emotion, but whatever they say may not always be true. As he appeared for the toss, Zorawar had a blank expression on his new grown full bearded face but it was evident that he had deliberately concealed every bit of emotion behind it, as if he was going to play a game of poker and not cricket. He squint his eyes and pushed the eyebrows together, then down and stared like an intelligent evil for a while into Monty's unassuming face, followed by a push of the lower jaw forward, perhaps trying to convey his inner intentions or maybe just to scare the opposition captain.

As expected, the umpires for the final were the most experienced ones – the sixty year old gymnast Mr. Francis and the most overpriced tailor of the town, Master Shams-ud-din. This was the first instance when Monty met the Master since the time he visited the Powerful horse boutique for the investigation of Scarlett's murder. The Master whooshed past him as if he was in his workplace instead of a public stadium and handed over the coin to Zorawar, forcing Monty to make a call within a split second. Heads was the call but it came down as tails. Zorawar opted to bat first. His face was now the one of triumph as both the captains jogged back to their respective dressing rooms without exchanging any words between them.

"Though he hates our coach, I can guarantee you that he will be fair throughout the match," said Sarfaraz, referring to his boss, Master Shams-ud-din but his teammates were still stubbornly skeptical about the umpire being biased. What they obviously missed the most were the golden words from Canada, who was until then in the washroom.

"No tips, no motivational quotes, no strategic advises, what sort of match is this going to be," said Beta as he dusted off the mud trapped between the spikes of his right shoe.

"We have made it to the final because we have the x-factor in us," replied Kunal as he jumped around the dressing room in order to warm up before the fielding stint.

"Yes, and we just need to continue doing what we have been doing since the first match," added Kamlesh as they walked out of the dressing room into the field.

"Woof, woof, woof," they yelled after Monty finished his five second conversation in the team huddle and they rushed to their allotted fielding positions.

Southern Blasters made a change in their batting line up. Instead of batting at three, much to the cheer of the crowd including Shefali, Zorawar came out to open the innings. He walked incredibly straight, keeping his chin up and eyes forward. Surprisingly, he wore a cap in place of the helmet, a dangerous but perhaps strategically motivated move to lower the confidence of the Brave Dogs' quickies.

In order to surprise the batsmen, Monty started with the left arm orthodox spin of Alpha. The first delivery spun away from the reach of the first opening batsman and he got beaten. Sooraj was alert to the cause and whipped off the bails in a jiffy. The batsman's foot dragged out slightly and he could not sneak back in time. In the absence of the third umpire, the standing umpire at square leg,

Master Shams-ud-din raised his finger declaring the batsman out. The start was like a dream for the Brave Dogs and also assured them that the umpire would not make any biased decisions throughout the course of the match.

Though the cheerleaders in red began their stuff with the fluffy pompoms, people were more interested in the game and avoided looking at the dancing men. Meanwhile Canada came out of the washroom, walked up to the dugout, clapped and then again rushed to the washroom, cursing Gulgule as much as any man could. The Brave Dogs were not pleased with the absence of their coach from the dugout but there was very little they could do to control someone's loose motions.

The next few overs were only about some classy power hitting from the fiery blade of Zorawar. He was on a no-mercy mode against all the bowlers, be it Alpha, Jaganbir, Pappu, the revenge seeking Beta or the debutant Ratandeep. The scorecard read 123/1 in 10 overs with Arvind on 19 and Zorawar on 94 and the rest of the runs were scored courtesy wide balls deliberately bowled to prevent sixes.

With the vice captain Kunal falling short of ideas, Monty was the sole in charge of the decisions made on the field and none went his way. Probably, each of those tactical decisions in his head turned out to be as heavy as the weight of infuriation that causes a torpedo inside the cranium of a father taking his own child to a hospital. Every eye of his own teammates turned his way in a barely concealed hope. Perhaps the worst time to be the captain had arrived and that too without a prior notice. He wanted to speak to the coach at least for a minute to help him set the fielding positions, to create a new strategy for picking up wickets, to guide him with respect to the bowling changes, but Canada was still in the washroom.

Meanwhile, in his attempt to complete a quick single, Arvind suffered a leg cramp. The game paused for some time as the physiotherapist came out to help the batsman with a couple of quick stretches. The Brave Dogs did not even bother to form a huddle. They stood in silence with their heads down at their designated fielding positions but Kalee jogged into the playing area carrying a water bottle and the spiral notebook of the coach.

"It is not possible that one would write for no reason. Though Sir is still in the washroom there might be some knowledge that can be transferred from his brain to yours if you can quickly read this notebook," said Kalee as he handed over the notebook to the captain and passed the water bottle to Kunal fielding at mid off.

Initially reluctant to turn a few pages, Monty realized that he did not have many options. It was not a large notebook or particularly thick, but inside lay the answer he had sought for a long time. Though it was not crammed with shorthand writing or crazy symbols, it contained a unique adjective or a phrase on every page and a players' name below it. With his brows knitting and several deep sighs escaping gently from his pristine lips, Monty's eyeballs began to move over the pages from left to right. The first adjective was egoistic and the name of the player was Kunal.

With his mind kicking over and over like the screen of a mobile whose battery was absolutely uncharged, Monty read the remaining pairs at the speed that a chef would be annoyed in, when asked to make dinner with bare cupboards: Standby – Ratandeep, Warrior – Alpha Kumar, Work in progress – Junaid, Filler - Kamlesh, Tranquil - Sooraj, Surprise Package - Sarfaraz, Panic creator – Jaganbir, Stylish Striker – Dipshit, Trump card – Pappu, Crisis man – Beta Kumar, Game changer – Kalee, Leader – Monty C Dhingra. The skipper quickly saw towards the pitch where the batsman had already made to his feet and then continued reading: The Pride of t20 cricket – Beta Kumar's name was struck off and now there was a mention of Zorawar Bagga, champions – Brave Dogs' name was struck off and now there was mention of Southern Blasters, Winner – My princess with a smiley wearing a crown!

An indecipherable, faint smile bent the captain's lips anticlockwise by not more than five degrees as Monty realized that the Brave Dogs had been betrayed not by their coach but by a father.

He knew that the coach had implicitly good faith in him and therefore his name was paired with the adjective leader. "A good leader is a good decision maker," he said to himself as the deep sighs changed into shallow ones of the newfound belief.

"You are not in the playing XI but you changed the final game, thanks," he said confidently to the confused twelfth man and handed over the notebook to him. Kalee jogged out of the playing area with the water bottle and the notebook as the game was ready to continue.

"Brave Dogs," the leader shouted and appallingly clapped thrice to make sure most of them look at him and then using his hands, requested them to change their positions, thereby changing the field to an aggressive leg side one from the preplanned defensive one.

"Jaganbir, you are bowling the eleventh over. We are switching to a new plan. This is just opposite to all those we have discussed. Aim at the leg stump and not outside off," he said as he handed over the ball to Jaganbir.

Monty could close his eyes and feel the positivity flow, recharging his neurons until they rekindled and sparked. That was the level of optimism that he had attained after reading the notebook. The other Brave Dogs took inspiration from their leader and prepared themselves to start with a new blaze.

Zorawar walked out of the crease, as if Jaganbir was a slow spinner, and pulled it away for a flat 70m six over the vacant deep square leg to reach his fourth consecutive century of the tournament, thereby becoming the first player in the history of ICC to achieve that unbelievable feat. The celebrations from the champion were neither intense nor spectacular. He simply raised his bat to acknowledge the fans and then suddenly blew a kiss towards Shefali, sitting in the third row of the A stand. It was exactly then that Monty saw Canada peeping from the door of the dressing room with his left hand still on his paunch and his right fist moving in an up and down manner like the hand of an experienced drummer. Shefali was not from the 1960s or 70s. She was from the 90s. She blew a kiss back and Zorawar accepted it by catching it and putting it back into his heart, next to the sponsor logo on his yellow jersey. Canada then ran into the dressing room, perhaps the washroom beckoning him once again.

The new plan worked well to some extent. The run rate dropped and they could manage to take three wickets too but Zorawar continued his faultless and unsparing hitting. The scorecard read 231/4 in 19 overs with Zorawar batting on 169, an individual score that had never been reached in any professional t20 match played at Kanpur.

Running out of options, and probably in a move to surprise the unstoppable batsman, Monty brought himself on to bowl the last over of the innings. Never during those lengthy practice sessions had he practiced the art of bowling. Even the other Brave Dogs did not know what he could do with the ball in hand. "Right arm medium, over the wicket," he said to Master Shams-ud-din as the latter lopsidedly smiled back, as if the umpire had just won a cricket match against the Brave Dogs.

Zorawar used his feet but due to the slowness of Monty's first delivery, he did not quite get to the pitch of the ball. Instead of timing, it was the use of maximum power that launched it all the way over wide long off for a six. The two captains, one down on his knees after bowling the effort ball, and the other standing still in admiration of his shot, locked eyes with each other. While the latter stood tall and straight like a brave soldier of the Indian army, the former's shoulders dropped considerably like those of a defeated enemy, but he tried his best not to show his helplessness to his counterpart. The press reporters took a couple of pictures of the dramatic visual, perhaps already thinking about the headline of the story for the next day's newspaper.

The next four deliveries too went flying into the crowd. The worst part about it was that all four disappeared in four different directions, making the crowd almost laugh at the substandard bowling from Monty. For the fielders, it was just a stand and watch type of phase as they had lost all hopes of catching or even reaching to the ball in order to stop it.

As the fat droplets of sweat poured down from the forehead, back of the head and the unshaven armpits of the bearded cheerleaders in yellow, the wicked DJ played one of the most popular Bollywood tracks from the early

90's, "Drop by drop comes down the rain and water ignites fire within." It was obvious that the three guys had totally suffered from dehydration while the ones in red had not lost even a single globule of moisture due to perspiration.

With Zorawar on 199, Monty ran in to bowl the last ball of the innings. Bowled at a mere 99kmph, it was a perfect yorker and even Zorawar could not do much about it. Though not aimed to perfection, it somehow travelled to the base of the off stump and crashed straight into the furniture. The yayyys changed to ooohs in the crowd as Monty became the first man to dismiss Zorawar in ICC 2020. The bearded cheerleaders in red finally got something to dance and cheer about but it was perhaps too late for them to celebrate.

As the players ran in to congratulate the record breaking batsman, Monty too patted on his back in a display of wholesome sportsmanship. Simple but evidently sincere appreciation for the excellent display of batting shined on Monty's skin like colorless beads of dew on the green grass in winters. The entire crowd was up on their feet, clapping and saluting, as Zorawar returned like a king returning after being victorious in a one-sided battle, followed by the Brave Dogs. The slump in their body language was a clear indication of the fact that they had already realized what a target of 262 in a final feels like even before the chase had started.

On the way up to his team's dressing room, Zorawar blew another kiss to Shefali. This time, the latter caught it and placed it securely in her heart, covering it with both her palms. Even though the result of the match was still a long time away, there was uninhibited euphoria in her heart, an emotional state that was missing from many days. It was perhaps a spark of hope, a feeling of optimism, the anticipation of some good things to come.

Brave Dogs' dressing room had a ghostlike quietness that some would define as deafening. Not counting the one in the washroom, there were thirteen humans in there but the only sound that they generated was of their breathing. They were not accustomed to the noise of silence. Every moment till then, Canada was there to raise their morale, to guide them, to tell them in clear words what to do next and how. He would sometimes even leak the opposition players' weaknesses and their strengths to help his boys adjust their game according to that. But, the day they needed him the most, he was not there to help.

After padding up, Sarfaraz noted that his shoe lace was not tied properly. Just as he bent to tie it, he felt a touch of a heavy hand on his depressed shoulder. He turned around to see that it was indeed the captain's hand. The entire team gathered around to listen to what Monty had to say. Looking at the bat in his own hand, he said, "The worst thing we can be at this moment is being opposite to what our name suggests. We got to be brave, not a bunch of cowards. Ready to die an emotional death, only a coward will sacrifice his self-esteem and quit fighting when the situation goes against him. The Brave Dogs have risen from the ashes and are here not just to compete, but to win." He then raised his volume to make sure that he is audible behind the closed door of the washroom too, "Someone locked himself in a toilet but we cannot lose a match in hope that he will be back to help us pull this through. I am going to play the next twenty overs for every person in red at the stadium today. I will give it all I have to make sure that none of my supporter is disappointed. I expect the same from my team too."

"We will give our best," replied the other teammates. Putting on the helmet, Kunal added, "Not even in a swimming pool, we have been trained in a bathtub and now suddenly thrown into an ocean and asked to swim. I think we all do not know exactly what to do."

"Woof, woof, woof," echoed the dressing room. Though the door of the washroom still remained closed, they could hear the coach shout, "Woof, woof, woof," from inside.

Monty said, "Beta will bat at three and Ratandeep will slog at four. I am opening with Kunal and hope to score thirteen runs per over. Based on the situation, we will keep shuffling the batting order."

There was a confidence, hard-won yet deep in the eyes of all the thirteen men and that anchored true self belief in their thoughts. They knew that the target was massive but they had made up their minds to do all they could in order to achieve it. In that rawness, in the absolute vulnerability, Monty and Kunal walked out to bat, with insatiable hunger for runs incessantly dripping out of their muscles.

As Monty prepared to take guard, he quickly glanced at the fans in red. His eyes squinted and mouth opened slightly in an expression of stunned surprise. Although he was staring straight at the crowd, Shefali did not appear anywhere among them. Perhaps she had gone to purchase some eatables he thought but was disturbed by Kunal, who said, "The bowler is planning to bowl on the middle stump line and might alter the length on all six deliveries."

"How do you know?"

"I am a mentalist!" said Kunal, followed by a deep and throaty chuckle.

The two batsmen punched each other's gloves as Mr. Francis said, "Play!"

The first delivery squirted past the leg stump after taking the inner edge of Monty's blade and ran quickly to the ropes, giving a nervous yet desired start to the Brave Dogs' chase. "It is white, round and weighs about 163g. Hit it properly if you can Mr. Fluke," the animated bowler was right into the face of the batting captain but the latter chose not to respond. He smashed the second ball right down the ground for another four, but this time with one of the cleanest bat swings. "You know what it looks like Mr. Cartoon, now go and fetch it!" he replied as the bowler returned to his mark with a face similar to that of a furious mouse caught in a wooden trap, the only difference being that he was not as squeaky as the real one.

Amidst the silence in the crowd, Monty heard a familiar female voice. After taking a brief look, he realized that she was Shefali. For the next two seconds, his body did not shake at all. The bowler once again bowled in middle stump line and good length area and he somehow managed to strike it, but not in the gap. "Red suits her more, father -1, boyfriend - 1," he murmured to himself at a volume equivalent to that of a homely girl who rejects a prospective groom in front of her parents. Shefali had changed her top to a red one with the bull dog logo in its centre, proving that she was there to support the Brave Dogs.

Meanwhile, Canada Singh came out of the washroom and was in charge of all the conversations in the dugout. "Guys, we need to chase this down scoring 13+ runs per over. That means at least two boundaries per over and no dot balls. We need to switch to the power hitting mode. I know the strength possessed by Ratandeep. I am promoting him to three." The Brave Dogs however were as silent as the chirpiest ones in their graves.

At the end of the first over, the scorecard read 13/0, giving an opportunity to Canada to try his best to motivate the players. "We have started in the best way possible. One over is done and dusted. Only 19 more left." Then he turned towards the crowd. Even after rubbing his eyes twice, Canada could not read the text on Shefali's top but clearly saw the bull dog logo. Her coming near Canada was forbidden but his staying away from her was a pain, intensely sickening pain. Though he was out to fill enthusiasm and a spirit of fight into his squad, he chose to return to the washroom.

When a player tries something beyond his natural game, very seldom does he succeed. The third delivery of the second over was full, fast and aimed straight at the base of the stumps. Monty was beaten for pace as he attempted to flick it on the leg side. It struck his left pad right in front of the off stump and Master Shams-ud-din did not have to think twice before raising his finger.

Shefali did not catch the flying kiss from the ecstatic Zorawar at the fall of the first Brave Dogs' wicket. Though it was a bit of a letdown, the skipper did not get too disheartened as he had ten others to celebrate with.

Beta and Ratandeep both tried to walk out to the middle, creating an out-an-out comic situation for the fiendish crowd but not for their captain. Taking his helmet off like a commando returning from a postponed mission, Monty pointed at Beta. The signal was clear enough for Ratandeep to return to the dugout. Obviously, Monty was not aware of the move planned by the peerless guru.

"He will bowl on the legs," said the wacko mentalist to the new batsman.

Taking the mercurial mind reading more seriously than it should have been, Beta Kumar exposed all his sticks by shuffling across but the bowler slipped in a slow full toss and Beta ended up playing all over it. The crisis man was bowled on a golden duck, pushing his team deeper into unprecedented crisis instead of pulling them out of it.

Perhaps done with the loose motions, Canada was back in the dugout but even the Punjabi genes found it tough to find words. Each and every Brave Dog sat stock still, expressionless and wordless in that dugout. Humans find it tough to react when a freakish holocaust strikes at the time when they are under prepared. And when they are completely unprepared, their reaction totally goes begging.

Kamlesh tried, Alpha tried, Ratandeep tried, Sarfaraz tried, Junaid tried, Sooraj tried, Jaganbir tried and even Pappu tried but apart from Kunal nobody could manage to be successful. Though he had one of the most horrendous days of his life with his mind reading tricks, the opening batsman carried the bat as they bundled out for a mere 61 in 8.4 overs, conceding a win by the biggest margin in history of ICC to the new champions, the Southern Blasters.

Barring Tanmey, Pornika, Sweety and Shefali, the entire crowd had already gone berserk. Most shrewd politicians believe that it is better to be in the opposite faction than to repeatedly hear own bloc's knell. The crowd seemed to be much influenced by those lawmakers. By the time of the fall of the last wicket, most people in red had switched in support of the yellow to witness the disastrous overthrowing of the Brave Dogs. If the defeat was humiliating, devastating and disgraceful, the crowd was sadistic, brutal and severely outspoken. Even the bearded cheerleaders in red seemed to enjoy their defeat.

Though her boyfriend's team had convincingly defeated the team of inexperienced boys created by her father, frankly, Shefali was not happy. Her three year old dream was going to turn into a beautiful, lifelong reality but she knew that her father's ten year old nightmare would turn more tireless at least for another year, perhaps even self-doubting.

Though the half witted conditions set by her father for her marriage had almost been fulfilled by her boyfriend, she was not content. Though she had worn a yellow top during the first innings, she was not cheerful. Though she genuinely loved her boyfriend a lot, clearly, she did not love her father any less. It was ten in a row for Canada and that was altogether an unpleasant shock for his beloved daughter too.

Somehow, she gathered moral courage to go down the fearfully steep stairs and into the ground. With each step, her mind became more confused, not like it used to be a day before her Physics examination but like that of a thirty eight year old spinster when teens refer to her as aunty. It felt as if the physical distance between the players and her increased instead of decreasing with every step she took closer to them.

As the faint light of the setting sun caressed her skin in order to promise the closure of a chapter and perhaps the beginning of a new one, she entombed her vivid memories of her carefree childhood and also the selfish ones of the previous three years. Pausing abruptly only to close her eyes and take in a deep breath of the pollinated air, she steeled herself to only think of her future from there on in. A future she would mould, build and direct. That thought gave more charge to her stride, more command to her own mind, body and soul. She was a girl walking into her own destiny, perhaps the one that lay squarely in her own decision. She reached the ground and stood still silently behind the backs of the players and others as the post match presentation ceremony commenced.

The umpire turned anchor, Master Shams-ud-din introduced the special guests including the ravishing couple of Hargurjeet and Anjana, and then said, "Before starting the post match presentation ceremony, I would like to apologize to Mr. CD Singh. Last year, I cooked up a false narrative in order to humiliate him because he insulted me during the match. He never had the intention to make his own team lose the match. Whatever he did was in excitement and love for the game."

Eyes turned towards the area where the Brave Dogs were standing but their esteemed coach was still not there. Perhaps he had gone to the washroom for one last time.

As the Master invited the losing captain, Monty walked towards the stage. His eyes did not follow his legs as they were locked with those of his counterpart. Perhaps that was his way of paying respect to the brutally intricate batting skills displayed by Zorawar. Some Southern Blasters' players thought that it was a look given by the brother of a bride to his brother-in-law and went on to pat on the back of their captain. However, Zorawar requested his players to keep calm and watch the proceedings.

Monty took the microphone in his own hands and said, "We are all from different backgrounds. Not even one of us is a contracted player. We tried our best to win the final but unfortunately our best was only second to the number one team. The result is completely acceptable as we are the brave ones who find success even in loss. For our incredible debut performance in ICC 2020, on the behalf of my entire team, I would like to give cent percent credit to our coach, manager, masseur, physiotherapist, consultant, strategic guru, mastermind, owner of the team, father like figure, caretaker, guide, friend, Canada Singh Sir. Every team had sponsors, doctors, managers but we had just one man. It is only because of him that thirteen rookies like us were on the playing field competing against some of the extra ordinarily talented teams, and not sitting somewhere in the crowd watching these hard fought matches with cold drink bottles in our hands. Thank you Sir for all you have given us. I regret that we could not win the trophy this year but I do assure you that we will work harder and come back stronger in the future to win and give it in your hands."

The other Brave Dogs could not agree more and clapped thunderously for their captain and coach.

Master Shams-ud-din then invited the winning captain, man of the match and the winner of The Pride of t20 cricket trophy, Zorawar Bagga. With the gold plated miniature stump and a bank cheque of 10lakh rupees in one of his hands and microphone in the other, he said, "My team and I were determined to play ruthless cricket today and end the game with a big win, especially after some of the unpleasant, off the field incidents. The communication between the management and the boys was transparent and uncomplicated. We were making it to the final every year and knew that our time would come sooner rather than later. On behalf of the entire Southern Blasters' family, I would like to credit our former coach Mr. Canada Singh for this glorious victory. He is the one who not only taught us the skills and gave us unbounded confidence to believe in our abilities, but also developed the art of overcoming perpetual challenges into each one of us. It is because of his hard work that Ayub Sir did not have much to do during his short stint with the team. I dedicate The Pride of t20 cricket trophy to my girlfriend Shefali and my team dedicates the ICC 2020 trophy to Canada Sir."

As Anjana presented the winning trophy to Zorawar, all members of his team jumped on the stage to pose with it. They had waited for seven years in a row for that moment. But, something was missing. Balloo ran into the dressing room of the Brave Dogs and when he came back, Canada Singh was with him.

Tears that well up, push together, and throw themselves over the rim of the eye. Canada had always been self-conscious when he cried, but then he just gave way to the enormity of his emotions. He himself did not know what made him cry, the emptiness and sorrow of losing the trophy for the tenth year in a row, the happiness and gratification of marrying his darling daughter to a champion or simply the satisfaction he derived after posing for a photograph with the winning team. Whatever it was, crying was necessary to cleanse his soul, perhaps a step to rediscover pride.

Meanwhile, the Brave Dogs marched into their dressing room, feeling proud of their newfound ICC runners up tag.

Devoid of any explanation, Shefali just shook her heavy head and the moment she began to cry, she knew that they were the tears of joy. She hugged her father and then her boyfriend in front of her father. She had no words to say but her fiancé did the talking on her behalf, "Though she was in yellow for the first half of the match, I knew she was here to support red. She wanted me to do well individually and then Brave Dogs to win the trophy. Sir, from this time on, I will not come to your house through the pipeline or like a mischievous thief from the balcony. My parents will come to meet you soon and talk about Shefali and my marriage."

"Had Southern Blasters lost today or had Zorawar not won The Pride of t20 cricket trophy, do you think I would have really married you to someone else? I am not an egoistic parent who would sit back, relax and watch his own child suffer," said Canada to his princess.

Shefali held Zorawar's hand tighter than before and replied, "Dad, I have inherited my genes from you. Do you think I would have really agreed to marry some other chap?"

What followed was spontaneous laughter on the faces of the couple and their father.

"You guys enjoy the victory, let me see what my boys are doing," said Canada as he jogged straight into the dressing room. Perhaps he wanted to let his team know that his stomach was actually upset and he never intended to make them lose the match.

As he reached the door of the dressing room, without making any kind of noise, he peeped inside, just like Jamal aunty used to peep out of her window.

Monty was saying to all his players, "Brave Dogs, each one of us came here naked with nothing to lose. We used, still use and will continue to use time to get baked. Maybe today was not our day, but soon we will come back stronger, wiser and with more passion to carry all before one!" The dressing room echoed with loud cheers from all the teammates, "You may think that we are the underdogs but no, no, no! We are the Brave Dogs, the mighty mighty Brave Dogs! Woof, woof, woof!"

Without entering inside, Canada also joined them, "Woof, woof, woof!"